PLASTIC CANVAS

Ultimate Christmas Companion™

Editorial Director: Donna Robertson
Production/Photography Director: Ange Van Arman
Product Development Manager: Fran Rohus

EDITORIAL
Senior Editor: Janet Tipton
Editor: Kris Kirst
Composing Editors: Jeanne Austin, Judy Crow,
Jaimie Davenport
Copy Editor: Salway Sabri
Copy Writer: Kim Votaw

PRODUCTION
Production Manager/Book Design: Debby Keel
Color Specialist: Betty Holmes
Production Coordinator: Glenda Chamberlain

PHOTOGRAPHY
Photography Manager: Scott Campbell
Photographers: Russell Chaffin, Keith Godfrey
Photography Coordinator/Stylist: Ruth Whitaker

PRODUCT DESIGN
Design Coordinator: Tonya Flynn

BUSINESS
C.E.O: John Robinson
Vice President/Marketing: Greg Deily

CREDITS
Sincerest thanks to all the designers, manufacturers and other professionals whose dedication has made this book possible. Special thanks to Quebecor Printing Book Group, Kingsport, TN.

Library of Congress Cataloging-in-Publication Data
ISBN: 1-57367-107-X
First Printing: 1999
Library of Congress Catalog Card Number: 99-74317

Published and Distributed by
The Needlecraft Shop, LLC, Big Sandy, Texas 75755
Printed in the United States of America.
www.needlecraftshop.com

Amber Beal

Dear Friend,

Children remind me of the true meaning and spirit of Christmas. For my friends, Amber and Micah, the holiday season is filled with surprises and wonders. Each four-year-old has an older brother, and the older boys – Trevor Godfrey and G.C. (short for Grover Cleveland III) Beal – play together on the same youth baseball team.

Amber's parents, Peggy and G.C. II, have established the tradition of opening gifts from family and friends Christmas eve, and saving presents from Santa for Christmas morning. Peggy remembers that last Christmas Amber expressed her delight each time she opened a gift by saying, "This is what I've been wanting all the time!"

Micah gets excited when his gifts include Power Rangers™ and Nintendo® games. His parents, Keith and Tammie Godfrey, took the boys to visit their grandparents in Oklahoma last Christmas. Tammie says Micah has yet to see and play in the snow, and hopes this winter a white Christmas can be enjoyed by all.

Amber and Micah are just beginning to write the stories of their lives. We hope you enjoy the little glimpses into our lives that we have included along-side a brand new gift-bag full of the most memorable plastic canvas ideas ever. May all your Christmas wishes come true!

Janet

Micah Godfrey

TABLE OF CONTENTS

Fireside Comforts for the Family

Lasting Memories for your Best Friend

Loving Touches for the Romantics

Tasty Creations for the Cook

Day Brighteners for your Co-Workers

Simple Pleasures for Special People

Growing Traditions for the Gardener

General Information

Fireside Comforts for the Family

Chapter One

Designed by Nancy Dorman

SIZE: Each snugly covers a boutique-style tissue box.

MATERIALS: Three sheets of 10-count plastic canvas; Six-strand embroidery floss (for amounts see Color Key); Medium metallic braid or six-strand metallic embroidery floss (for amount see Color Key); 3-ply or sport-weight yarn (for amounts see Color Key).

CUTTING INSTRUCTIONS:
NOTE: Graphs continued on page 10.
A: For Mrs. Claus sides, cut four 45 x 57 holes.
B: For Mr. Claus sides, cut four 45 x 57 holes.

C: For tops, cut two according to graph.

STITCHING INSTRUCTIONS:
1: Using yarn and braid or six strands metallic floss in colors and stitches indicated, work pieces according to graphs; fill in uncoded areas using holly and Continental Stitch. Using red and Herringbone Overcast, Overcast cutout edges of C pieces.
2: Using six strands floss in colors and embroidery stitches in indicated, embroider detail on A and B pieces as indicated on graphs.
3: For each Cover, using red and Herringbone Whipstitch, Whipstitch corresponding sides and one B together; with

8

Herringbone Overcast, Overcast unfinished bottom edges.

NOTE: Cut four 9" [22.9cm] lengths each of red floss and gold metallic braid or floss.

4: Tie each 9" strand into a small bow and trim ends. Glue one red bow to hair and one metallic bow to gift package on each side of Mrs. Claus Cover as shown in photo.‡

COLOR KEY: North Pole Tissues

Embroidery floss	AMOUNT
■ Green	7 yds. [6.4m]
■ Red	5 yds. [4.6m]
■ Pink	3 yds. [2.7m]
■ Blue	2 yds. [1.8m]

Metallic braid or floss	AMOUNT
□ Gold	6 yds. [5.5m]

Sport-weight	YARN AMOUNT
□ Holly	5 oz. [141.8g]
▨ Red	3 oz. [85.1g]
▨ White	26 yds. [23.8m]
■ Black	7 yds. [6.4m]
▨ Flesh Tone	5 yds. [4.6m]
▨ Crimson	3 yds. [2.7m]

STITCH KEY:

- — Backstitch/Straight
- ● French Knot

A – Mrs. Claus Side
(cut 4) 45 x 57 holes

TALES & FOLKLORE

Mrs. Claus is often overlooked during the holidays, but just where and how does she fit into the Christmas picture? According to some friendly and informative elves, Mrs. Claus' name is Clara and she helps Santa by making all kinds of goodies to feed him and his elfish helpers while they toil away in the workshops. Mrs. Claus also helps read Santa's letters and even answers some of them. In addition to all of this, she offers her input on gifts for the good boys and girls. Some naughty elves reported that Santa makes her clean out the reindeer stables, but I don't think that's true. According to more reliable eye-witnesses, that job was left for the Grinch™.

NORTH POLE TISSUES

(Instructions & photo on pages 8 & 9.)

Tip

These tissue covers will do double duty as planters or candy holders, if you stitch a bottom for them rather than a top.

B – Mr. Claus Side
(cut 4) 45 x 57 holes

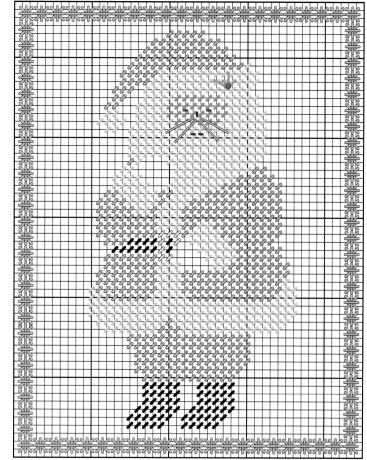

C – Top
(cut 2) 45 x 45 holes

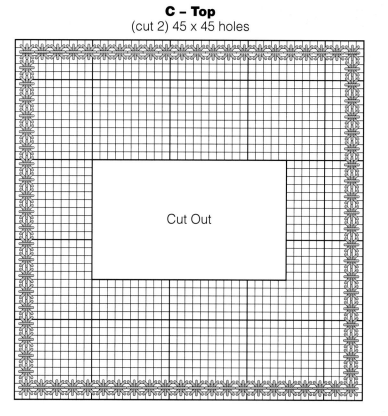

Cut Out

COLOR KEY: North Pole Tissues

Embroidery floss	AMOUNT
Green	7 yds. [6.4m]
Red	5 yds. [4.6m]
Pink	3 yds. [2.7m]
Blue	2 yds. [1.8m]

Metallic braid or floss	AMOUNT
Gold	6 yds. [5.5m]

Sport- weight	YARN AMOUNT
Holly	5 oz. [141.8g]
Red	3 oz. [85.1g]
White	26 yds. [23.8m]
Black	7 yds. [6.4m]
Flesh Tone	5 yds. [4.6m]
Crimson	3 yds. [2.7m]

STITCH KEY:
- Backstitch/Straight
- French Knot

SNOWMAN BASKET

Designed by
Chris Westerberg

Instructions on
next page

SNOWMAN BASKET

(Photo on page 11.)

SIZE: 2⅛" x 10¾" x 12¾" [5.4cm x 27.3cm x 32.4cm].

MATERIALS: Two sheets of 7-count plastic canvas; Craft glue or glue gun; Worsted-weight or plastic canvas yarn (for amounts see Color Key).

CUTTING INSTRUCTIONS:
NOTE: Graphs continued on page 14.
A: For back, cut one according to graph.
B: For front, cut one according to graph.
C: For sides, cut two 13 x 22 holes.

D: For bottom, cut one 13 x 48 holes (no graph).
E: For hat, cut one according to graph.

STITCHING INSTRUCTIONS:
NOTE: D piece is not worked.
1: Using colors and stitches indicated, work A-C and E pieces according to graphs. With matching colors, Overcast edges of E.
2: Whipstitch A-D pieces together as indicated on graphs and according to Basket Assembly Diagram on page 14. Glue hat to head as shown in photo.
3: Hang or display as desired.✤

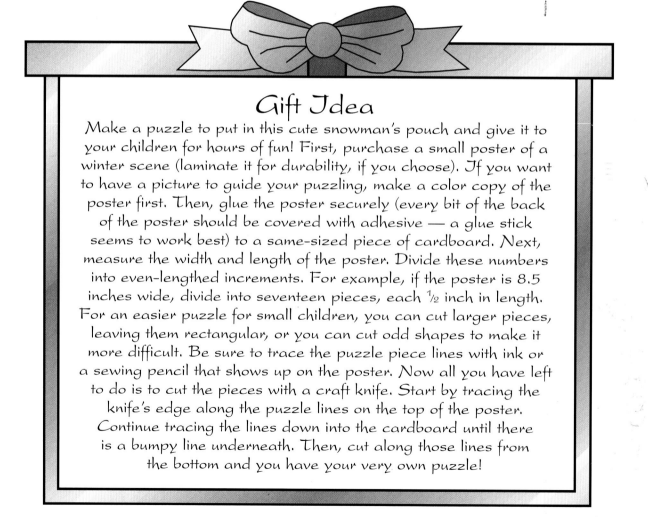

Gift Idea

Make a puzzle to put in this cute snowman's pouch and give it to your children for hours of fun! First, purchase a small poster of a winter scene (laminate it for durability, if you choose). If you want to have a picture to guide your puzzling, make a color copy of the poster first. Then, glue the poster securely (every bit of the back of the poster should be covered with adhesive — a glue stick seems to work best) to a same-sized piece of cardboard. Next, measure the width and length of the poster. Divide these numbers into even-lengthed increments. For example, if the poster is 8.5 inches wide, divide into seventeen pieces, each ½ inch in length. For an easier puzzle for small children, you can cut larger pieces, leaving them rectangular, or you can cut odd shapes to make it more difficult. Be sure to trace the puzzle piece lines with ink or a sewing pencil that shows up on the poster. Now all you have left to do is to cut the pieces with a craft knife. Start by tracing the knife's edge along the puzzle lines on the top of the poster. Continue tracing the lines down into the cardboard until there is a bumpy line underneath. Then, cut along those lines from the bottom and you have your very own puzzle!

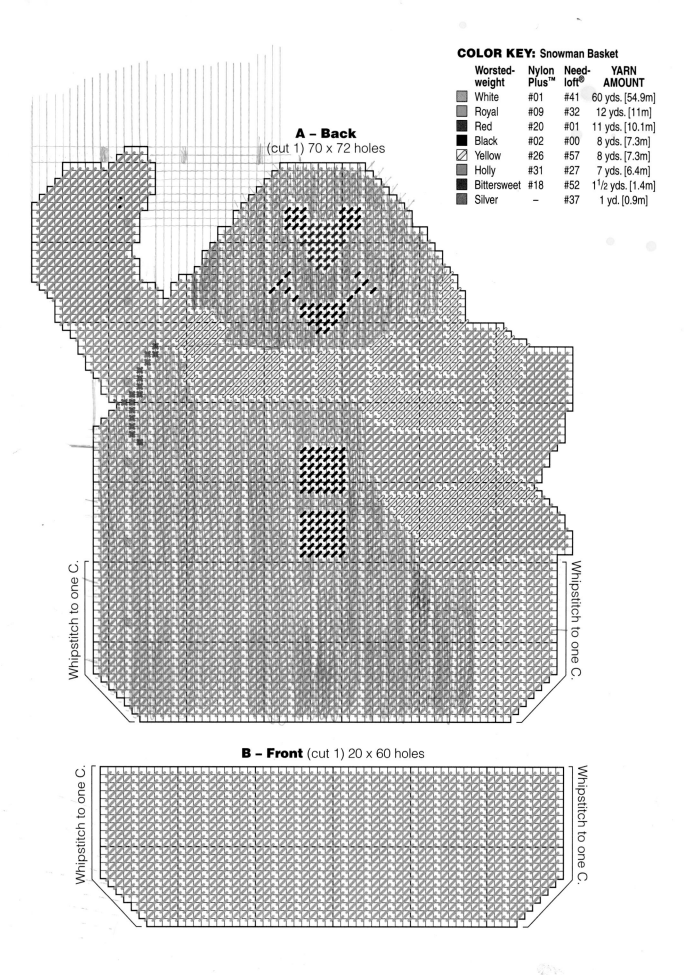

COLOR KEY: Snowman Basket

Worsted-weight	Nylon Plus™	Need-loft®	YARN AMOUNT
White	#01	#41	60 yds. [54.9m]
Royal	#09	#32	12 yds. [11m]
Red	#20	#01	11 yds. [10.1m]
Black	#02	#00	8 yds. [7.3m]
Yellow	#26	#57	8 yds. [7.3m]
Holly	#31	#27	7 yds. [6.4m]
Bittersweet	#18	#52	1½ yds. [1.4m]
Silver	–	#37	1 yd. [0.9m]

A – Back
(cut 1) 70 x 72 holes

Whipstitch to one C.

Whipstitch to one C.

B – Front (cut 1) 20 x 60 holes

Whipstitch to one C.

Whipstitch to one C.

SNOWMAN BASKET

(Instructions & photo on pages 11 & 12.)

E – Hat (cut 1) 28 x 35 holes

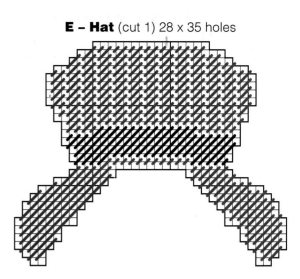

C – Side
(cut 2) 13 x 22 holes

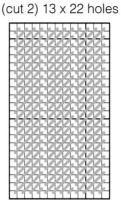

COLOR KEY: Snowman Basket

	Worsted-weight	Nylon Plus™	Need-loft®	YARN AMOUNT
	White	#01	#41	60 yds. [54.9m]
	Royal	#09	#32	12 yds. [11m]
	Red	#20	#01	11 yds. [10.1m]
	Black	#02	#00	8 yds. [7.3m]
	Yellow	#26	#57	8 yds. [7.3m]
	Holly	#31	#27	7 yds. [6.4m]
	Bittersweet	#18	#52	1½ yds. [1.4m]
	Silver	–	#37	1 yd. [0.9m]

Basket Assembly Diagram
(Pieces are shown in different colors for contrast.)

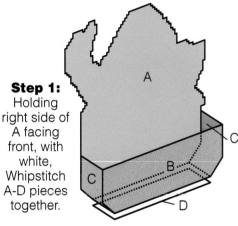

Step 1:
Holding right side of A facing front, with white, Whipstitch A-D pieces together.

Step 2:
With matching colors, Overcast unfinished edges.

Tip

Melt Scrooge's heart with this snowy guy. Hang him on your door to put holiday wishes in or to display an inspirational saying. You could even hang him on your refrigerator to hold note paper.

CHRISTMAS CLASSIC

Designed by
Michele Wilcox

Instructions on next page

Tip

Start a family tradition with this gift-within-a-gift. Open the front cover/lid to fill the container with a book your family will cherish for years to come, a VHS movie, popcorn, Christmas cookies, candles or ornaments. Afterwards, use it to store photos or stationery.

CHRISTMAS CLASSIC

(Photo on page 15.)

SIZE: 2½" x 6¼" x 9¼" [6.4cm x 15.9cm x 23.5cm].

MATERIALS: 2½ sheets of 7-count plastic canvas; Craft glue or glue gun; #3 pearl cotton or six-strand embroidery floss (for amounts see Color Key); Worsted-weight or plastic canvas yarn (for amounts see Color Key).

CUTTING INSTRUCTIONS:
A: For cover lid and bottom, cut two (one for lid and one for bottom) 41 x 61 holes (no bottom graph).
B: For cover spine, cut one 16 x 61 holes.
C: For box long sides, cut two 14 x 57 holes (no graph).
D: For box short sides, cut two 14 x 37 holes (no graph).

E: For box bottom, cut one 37 x 57 holes (no graph).

STITCHING INSTRUCTIONS:
1: Using colors and stitches indicated, work one A for lid and B pieces according to graphs; work remaining A for Cover bottom (substitute forest for gold) and E according to Cover & Box Bottom Stitch Pattern Guide. Fill in uncoded areas of lid A and B pieces using forest and Continental Stitch; using gold and Continental Stitch, work C and D pieces.
2: Using pearl cotton or six strands floss in colors and embroidery stitches indicated, embroider detail on lid A as indicated on graph.
3: Whipstitch and assemble pieces as indicated and according to Box Assembly Diagram.✢

Heartwarming Story

During the holidays, one of our family traditions when I was growing up was to gather around the living room and listen to my mother read to us out of our favorite books, one of which was <u>The Complete Works of Edward Lear</u>. We were so impressed with Lear's tales and limericks, that we would make up word plays for every special occasion that we could. In college, I was known as the "Limerick Girl," because I continued our family tradition with my friends and acquaintances. Now, when our family gets together, even though it's less often than we'd like, we sometimes reflect on the stories and tales we cherished most, and of course, one of us provides a suitable limerick. – Kim Votaw

A – Cover Lid (cut 1) 41 x 61 holes

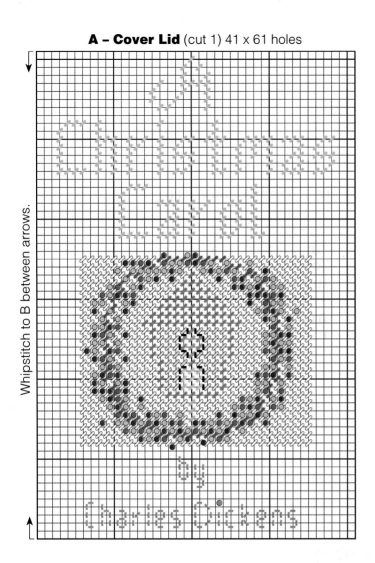

Whipstitch to B between arrows.

B – Cover Spine
(cut 1) 16 x 61 holes

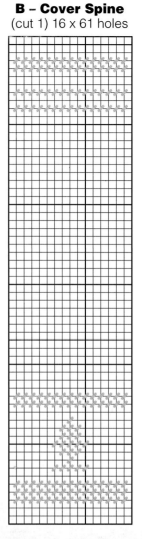

COLOR KEY: Christmas Classic

Pearl cotton or floss	AMOUNT
☐ Green	5 yds. [4.6m]
■ Mint	5 yds. [4.6m]
■ Olive	5 yds. [4.6m]
■ Red	4 yds. [3.7m]
■ Gold	3 yds. [2.7m]
■ Black	1 yd. [0.9m]

Worsted-weight	Nylon Plus™	Need-loft®	YARN AMOUNT
☐ Forest	#32	#29	3 oz. [85.1g]
☐ Gold	#27	#17	2¹/₂ oz. [70.9g]
☒ Eggshell	#24	#39	12 yds. [11m]
■ Xmas Green	#58	#28	3 yds. [2.7m]
■ Black	#02	#00	2 yds. [1.8m]
☒ Yellow	#26	#57	1¹/₂ yds. [1.4m]
☐ Red	#20	#01	¹/₂ yd. [0.5m]
☐ Bittersweet	#18	#52	¹/₄ yd. [0.2m]
☐ Tangerine	#15	#11	¹/₄ yd. [0.2m]

STITCH KEY:
- — Backstitch/Straight
- ● French Knot

Cover & Box Bottom Stitch Pattern Guide

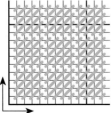

Continue established pattern up and across each entire piece.

Box Assembly Diagram
(Gray denotes wrong side.)

Step 1:
(inside view)
For cover, with forest, Whipstitch A and B pieces together; Overcast unfinished edges.

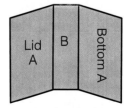

Step 2:
For box, with gold, Whipstitch C and D pieces wrong sides together and to right side of E; Overcast unfinished edges.

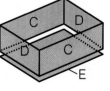

Step 3:
Glue box to spine and to center bottom of A.

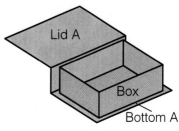

MUG INSERTS

MUG INSERTS

Designed by
Angie K. Arickx

SIZE: Each fits inside a 4"-tall [10.2cm] plastic snap-together mug.

MATERIALS FOR ONE: ½ sheet of 10-count plastic canvas; Snap-together mug; #3 pearl cotton or six-strand embroidery floss (for amounts see individual Color Keys; double amounts for floss).

CUTTING INSTRUCTIONS:
For Insert, cut one 34 x 97 holes.

STITCHING INSTRUCTIONS:
NOTE: Use pearl cotton or 12 strands embroidery floss throughout.
1: Using colors indicated and Continental Stitch, work Insert according to graph of choice; fill in uncoded areas using white and Continental Stitch.
2: With white, Whipstitch short ends of Insert together; Overcast unfinished edges. Place Insert inside mug according to manufacturer's instructions.‡

Gift Idea

Give someone you love a festive treat of these mug inserts this holiday season. Fill the mugs with candy, flavored teas and cocoas, sunflower seeds or raisins. Give your loving parents a "his & hers" set of these mugs with matching, stitched cutouts of the words "Mom" and "Dad" glued on the sides of plastic bowls. They can then fill the bowls with popcorn or their favorite snacks.

COLOR KEY: "Dad" Insert

#3 pearl cotton or floss	DMC®	Anchor®	JPC®	AMOUNT
White (blanc)	White	#02	#1002	28 yds. [25.6m]
Med. Delft Blue	#799	#136	#7030	18 yds. [16.5m]
Dk. Salmon	#3328	#1024	#3071	12 yds. [11m]
Dk. Royal Blue	#796	#133	#7100	11 yds. [10.1m]
Med. Garnet	#815	#43	#3000	6 yds. [5.5m]

COLOR KEY: "Mom" Insert

#3 pearl cotton or floss	DMC®	Anchor®	JPC®	AMOUNT
White (blanc)	White	#02	#1002	28 yds. [25.6m]
Salmon	#760	#1022	#3069	22 yds. [20.1m]
Vy. Dk. Salmon	#347	#1025	#3013	12 yds. [11m]
Vy. Dk. Emerald Green	#909	#923	#6228	8 yds. [7.3m]

"Dad" Insert (cut 1) 34 x 97 holes

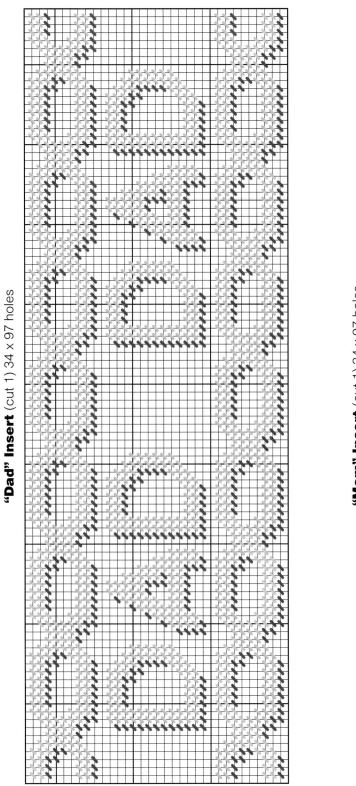

"Mom" Insert (cut 1) 34 x 97 holes

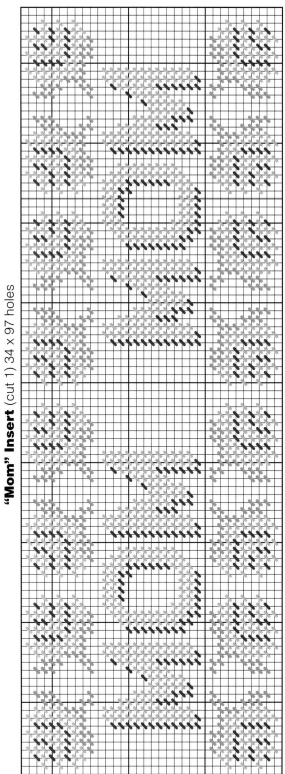

FIREPLACE CARD HOLDER

Designed by Nancy Dorman

Gift Idea

Give this special holder with a hand-picked Christmas card for your friend, or turn it into a gift box filled with candles or a book for fireside reading.

SIZE: 4½" x 10¾" x 8½" tall [11.4cm x 27.3cm x 21.6cm].

MATERIALS: Four sheets of 7-count and ½ sheet of 10-count plastic canvas; ¾ yd. [0.7m] of ¾" [1.9cm] artificial pine garland; Two ⅜" [10mm] jingle bells; 2¼ yds. [2.1m] red ⅛" [3mm] satin ribbon; Nine gold 3mm beads; Three 1½" [3.8cm] cinnamon sticks; Miniature flocked teddy bear; Four red artificial berry stamens; Four miniature decorative gift packages; Craft glue or glue gun; Medium metallic braid or six-strand metallic embroidery floss (for amount see Color Key on page 23); Six-strand embroidery floss (for amount see Color Key); Worsted-weight or plastic canvas yarn (for amounts see Color Key).

CUTTING INSTRUCTIONS:
NOTES: Graphs on pages 22 & 23. Use 10-count for K-M and 7-count canvas for remaining pieces.

A: For back, cut one according to graph.

B: For front, cut one according to graph.

C: For sides, cut two 17 x 29 holes.

D: For base, cut one according to graph.

E: For mantel top, cut one according to graph.

F: For mantel front, cut one 3 x 62 holes (no graph).

G: For mantel sides, cut two 3 x 19 holes (no graph).

H: For interior back, cut one 16 x 19 holes (no graph).

I: For interior sides, cut two 5 x 16 holes (no graph).

J: For interior top, cut one 5 x 19 holes (no graph).

K: For andirons, cut two according to graph.

L: For small stockings, cut two according to graph.

M: For large stocking, cut one according to graph.

STITCHING INSTRUCTIONS:
1: Using colors and stitches indicated, work A-E pieces according to graphs. Using brown and Slanted Gobelin Stitch over narrow width, work F and G pieces; using dk. gray and Continental Stitch, work H-J pieces.

2: With pewter, Overcast edges of D piece. Using six strands floss and Backstitch, embroider detail on A-C pieces as indicated on graphs.

NOTE: Use Herringbone Whipstitch and Herringbone Overcast for fireplace assembly.

3: Whipstitch and assemble A-J pieces as indicated and according to Fireplace Assembly Diagram on page 23.

NOTE: Separate red, green and white worsted yarn into 2-ply or nylon plastic canvas yarn into 1-ply strands.

4: Using 2-ply (or 1-ply) yarn and a doubled strand of braid or 12 strands metallic floss in colors indicated and Continental Stitch, work K-M pieces according to graphs; with matching colors, Overcast edges. Using yarn in colors indicated and Backstitch, embroider detail on L and M pieces as indicated.

5: Drape and glue garland around sides and front of mantel as shown in photo, trimming as needed to fit. Shape remaining garland into a wreath and glue to back of fireplace as shown.

NOTE: Cut five 9" [22.9cm] lengths of ribbon.

6: Tie each 9" ribbon into a small bow; trim ends as desired. Glue one bow and one bell to garland at each front corner of mantel (see photo); glue remaining bows and stockings to garland across front as shown. Tie remaining ribbon into a multiloop bow and glue to wreath.

7: Glue beads to garland between bells and stockings; glue stamens and remaining beads evenly spaced around wreath as shown or as desired.

8: Glue cinnamon sticks together and to interior of fireplace, and glue andirons as indicated to base in front of sticks as shown. Glue bear and gift packages to base at front of fireplace as desired or as shown.✢

FIREPLACE CARD HOLDER

(Instructions & photo on pages 20 & 21.)

K – Andiron
(cut 2 from 10-count)
8 x 8 holes

Glue

L – Small Stocking
(cut 2 from 10-count)
6 x 10 holes

Tip

A warm addition to your family atmosphere is here in this cozy fireplace container. You can put your journal, stamps, paper and pens in it, or place it by the fireplace to hold long matches.

A – Back
(cut 1 from 7-count) 55 x 59 holes

M – Large Stocking
(cut 1 from 10-count)
7 x 12 holes

C – Side
(cut 2 from 7-count)
17 x 29 holes

B – Front
(cut 1 from 7-count) 29 x 59 holes

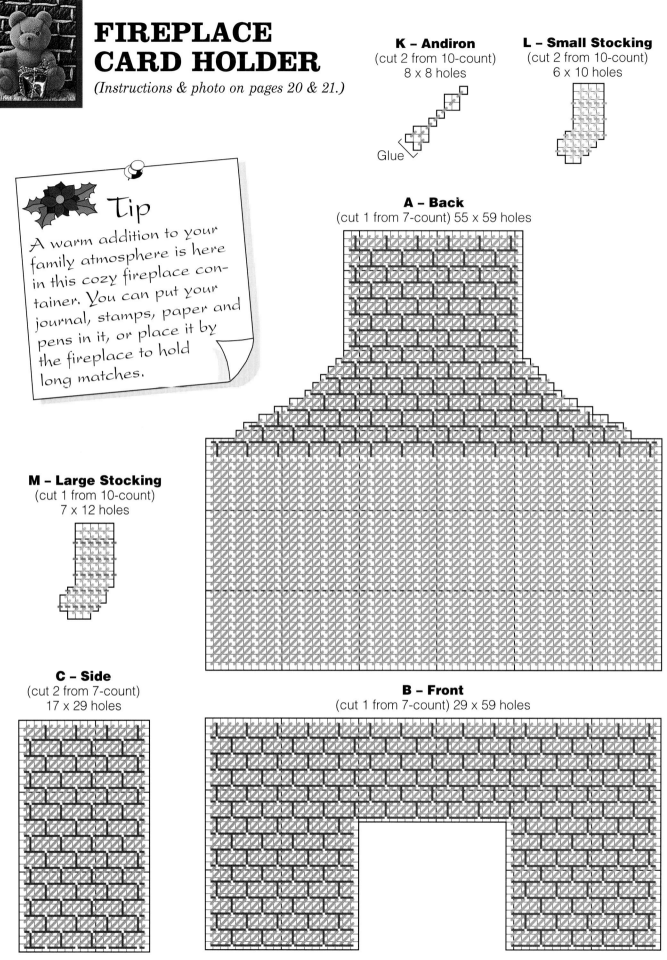

Metallic braid or floss			AMOUNT
■ Gold			4 yds. [3.7m]

Embroidery floss			AMOUNT
■ Lt. Gray			40 yds. [36.6m]

Worsted-weight	Nylon Plus™	Need-loft®	YARN AMOUNT
■ Cinnamon	#44	#14	3 oz. [85.1g]
■ Pewter	#40	#65	50 yds. [45.7m]
■ Brown	#36	#15	25 yds. [22.9m]
□ Dk. Gray	–	–	10 yds. [9.1m]
■ Xmas Red	#19	#02	3 yds. [2.7m]
■ Xmas Green	#58	#28	2 yds. [1.8m]
■ White	#01	#41	1 yd. [0.9m]

STITCH KEY:

- — Backstitch/Straight
- □ Fireplace Attachment

Fireplace Assembly Diagram

(Pieces are shown in different colors for contrast; gray denotes wrong side.)

Step 1:
(back view)
With dk. gray, Whipstitch H-J pieces right sides together; with cinnamon, Whipstitch interior to opening on wrong side of A.

Step 2:
With dk. gray, Overcast bottom edges of interior.

Step 3:
Holding right side of back facing in, with cinnamon, Whipstitch A-C pieces together, forming fireplace; Overcast unfinished edges.

Step 4:
Tack fireplace to right side of D.

Step 5:
With brown, Whipstitch E-G pieces together; Overcast unfinished edges.

Step 6:
Glue mantel over top edge of fireplace front and sides.

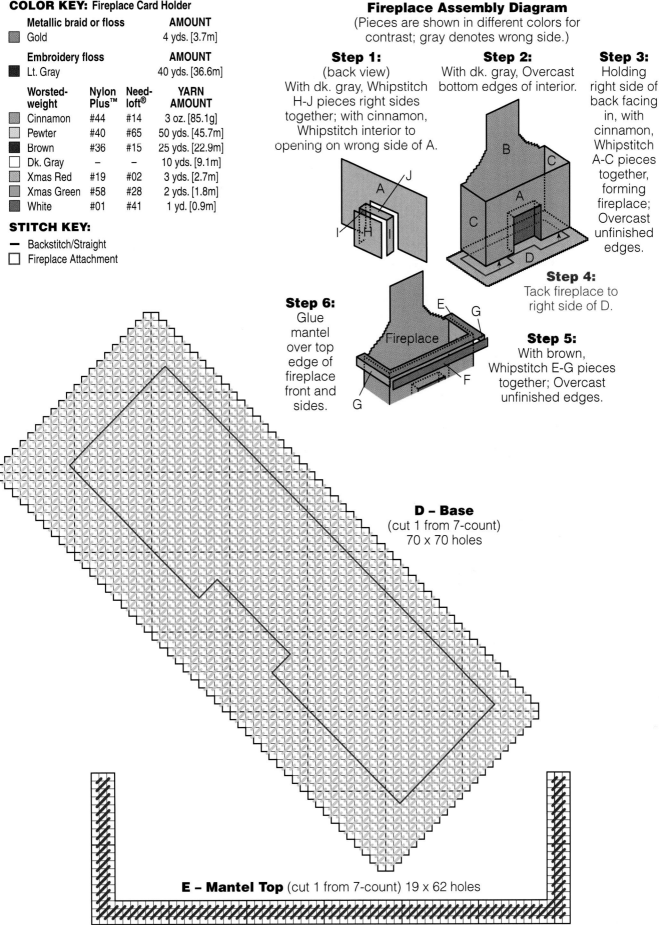

D – Base
(cut 1 from 7-count)
70 x 70 holes

E – Mantel Top (cut 1 from 7-count) 19 x 62 holes

Designed by Joyce Keklock

SIZE: Decorates a 14" [35.6cm] wreath.

MATERIALS: One 12" x 18" [30.5cm x 45.7cm] or larger sheet of 7-count plastic canvas; 14" [35.6cm] grapevine wreath; 1 yd. [0.9m] red with gold metallic edging 1½" [3.8cm] wire-edged ribbon; Craft glue or glue gun; Worsted-weight or plastic canvas yarn (for amounts see Color Key.)

CUTTING INSTRUCTIONS:

A: For Picture, cut one according to graph.

B: For gingerbread men, cut number indicated according to graphs on page 26.

STITCHING INSTRUCTIONS:

1: Using colors and stitches indicated, work pieces according to graphs; with matching colors, Overcast edges.

2: Using colors (Separate into individual plies, if desired.) and embroidery stitches indicated, embroider detail on pieces as indicated on graphs.

3: Glue A to back and B pieces to front of wreath as shown in photo. Tie ribbon into a bow and glue to center top of wreath as shown.

4: Hang as desired.✝

COLOR KEY: Gingerbread Wreath

	Worsted-weight	Nylon Plus™	Need-loft®	YARN AMOUNT
	Sail Blue	#04	#35	45 yds. [41.1m]
	White	#01	#41	40 yds. [36.6m]
	Maple	#35	#13	39 yds. [35.7m]
	Holly	#31	#27	14 yds. [12.8m]
	Black	#02	#00	12 yds. [11m]
	Xmas Red	#19	#02	12 yds. [11m]
	Fern	#57	#23	4 yds. [3.7m]
	Forest	#32	#29	3 yds. [2.7m]
	Lemon	#25	#20	2 yds. [1.8m]
	Lilac	#22	#45	1 yd. [0.9m]
	Pink	#11	#07	1 yd. [0.9m]

STITCH KEY:

— Backstitch/Straight
● French Knot

A – Picture (cut 1) 78 x 78 holes

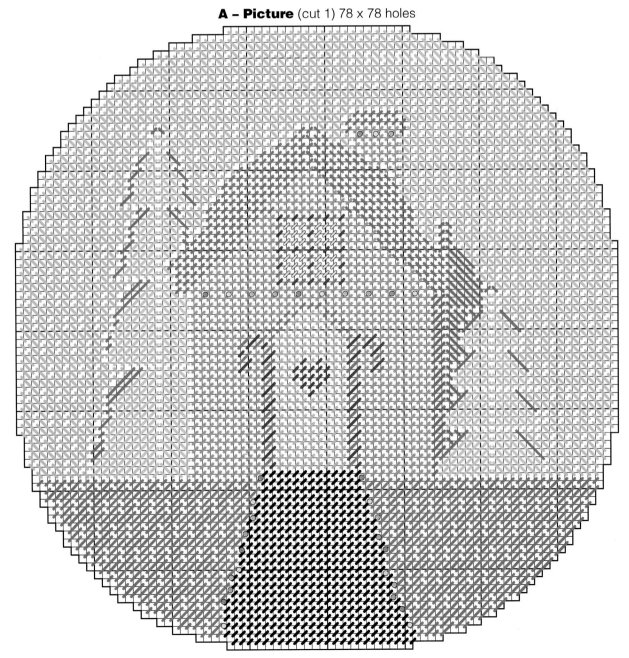

Fireside Comforts For The Family

GINGERBREAD WREATH

(Instructions & photo on pages 24 & 25.)

B – Gingerbread Man "W"
(cut 1) 17 x 17 holes

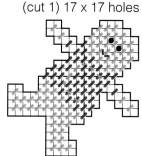

B – Gingerbread Man "E"
(cut 2) 17 x 17 holes

B – Gingerbread Man "L"
(cut 1) 17 x 17 holes

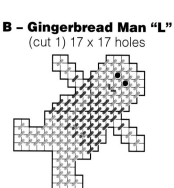

B – Gingerbread Man "C"
(cut 1) 17 x 17 holes

COLOR KEY: Gingerbread Wreath

	Worsted-weight	Nylon Plus™	Need-loft®	YARN AMOUNT
	Sail Blue	#04	#35	45 yds. [41.1m]
	White	#01	#41	40 yds. [36.6m]
	Maple	#35	#13	39 yds. [35.7m]
	Holly	#31	#27	14 yds. [12.8m]
	Black	#02	#00	12 yds. [11m]
	Xmas Red	#19	#02	12 yds. [11m]
	Fern	#57	#23	4 yds. [3.7m]
	Forest	#32	#29	3 yds. [2.7m]
	Lemon	#25	#20	2 yds. [1.8m]
	Lilac	#22	#45	1 yd. [0.9m]
	Pink	#11	#07	1 yd. [0.9m]

STITCH KEY:

— Backstitch/Straight
● French Knot

B – Gingerbread Man "O"
(cut 1) 17 x 17 holes

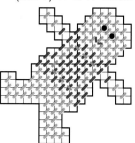

B – Gingerbread Man "M"
(cut 1) 17 x 17 holes

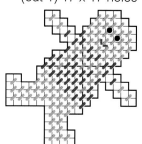

POINSETTIA BELLS

Designed by
Patricia Hall

Instructions on next page

POINSETTIA BELLS

(Photo on page 27.)

SIZES: Wall Motif is 11⅛" x 13¼" [28.3cm x 33.7cm], not including hanger; each Coaster is 4¾" x 5¼" [12.1cm x 13.3cm]; Ornament is 3⅜" x 3⅞" [8.6cm x 9.8cm], not including hanger.

MATERIALS: Two 12" x 18" [30.5cm x 45.7cm] or larger sheets of 7-count plastic canvas; Two standard-size sheets of 7-count plastic canvas; 1 yd. [0.9m] gold metallic ¼" [6mm] twisted cord; 2¼ yds. [2.1m] gold metallic ⅛" [3mm] wire rattail ribbon; 1 yd. [0.9m] gold fine metallic braid or metallic floss; 2 yds. [1.8m] gold metallic 2" [5.1cm] wire-edged mesh ribbon; #3 pearl cotton or six-strand embroidery floss (for amount see Color Key); Uniek® metallic cord (for amount see Color Key); Worsted-weight or plastic canvas yarn (for amounts see Color Key).

CUTTING INSTRUCTIONS:

NOTE: Use large sheets for A pieces.
A: For Wall Motif front and backing, cut two (one for front and one for backing) according to graph.
B: For Coaster fronts and backings, cut eight (four for fronts and four for backings) according to graph.
C: For Ornament sides, cut two according to graph.

STITCHING INSTRUCTIONS:

NOTE: One A and four B pieces are not worked for backings.
1: Using pearl cotton or six strands floss, metallic cord and yarn in colors and stitches indicated, work one A piece for front, four B pieces for fronts and C pieces according to graphs.
2: For Wall Motif, glue twisted cord across lower right side of front A as shown in photo, trimming away excess as needed and gluing ends to wrong side to secure.
3: Holding backing A to wrong side of

front A with ends of remaining twisted cord between at center top for hanger, with matching colors, Whipstitch together.
4: Glue rattail ribbon across lower right side of each front B piece and across lower right side of one C piece as shown, trimming away excess as needed and gluing ends to wrong side to secure.
NOTE: Cut five 6" [15.2cm] lengths of fine metallic braid or metallic floss; knot ends of each cut strand together, forming hangers.
5: For each Coaster, holding one backing B to wrong side of one front B with one hanger between at center top, with matching colors, Whipstitch together. For Ornament, holding C pieces wrong sides together with remaining hanger between at center top, Whipstitch together.
NOTE: Cut five 12" [22.9cm] lengths of rattail ribbon; tie each ribbon into a bow.
6: Glue one rattail ribbon bow to Ornament and to each Coaster as shown or as desired. Tie mesh ribbon into a multiloop bow as desired and glue to top of Wall Motif as shown.✝

B – Coaster Front & Backing
(cut 4 each) 31 x 34 holes

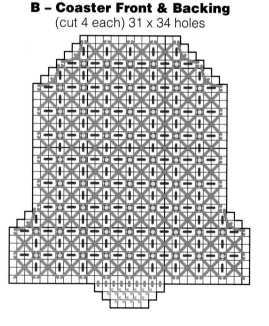

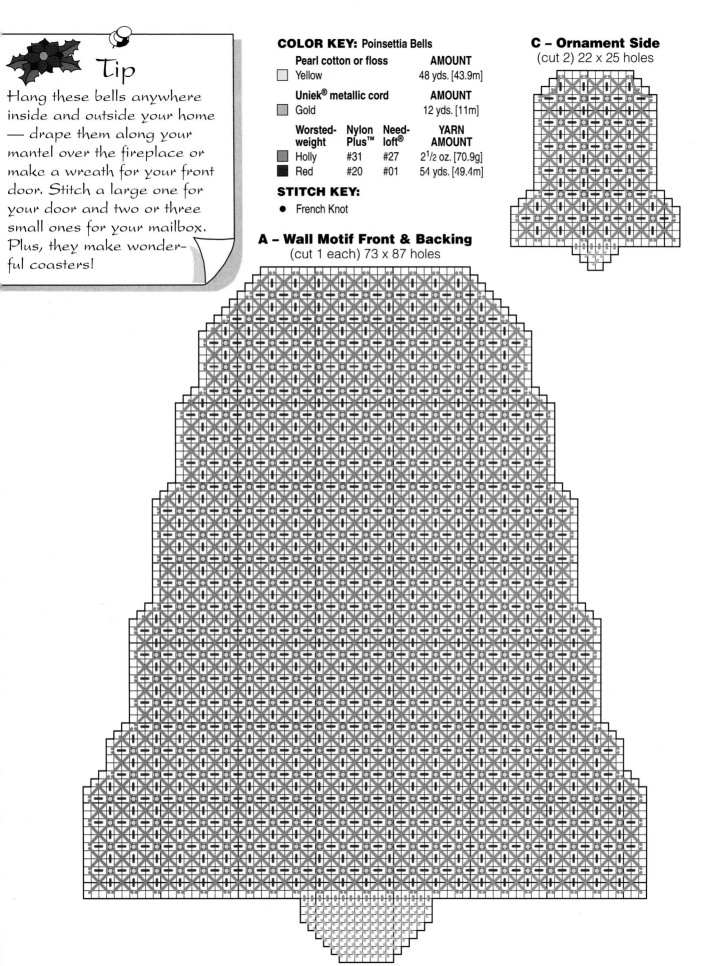

Tip

Hang these bells anywhere inside and outside your home — drape them along your mantel over the fireplace or make a wreath for your front door. Stitch a large one for your door and two or three small ones for your mailbox. Plus, they make wonderful coasters!

COLOR KEY: Poinsettia Bells

Pearl cotton or floss			AMOUNT
☐ Yellow			48 yds. [43.9m]
Uniek® metallic cord			**AMOUNT**
☐ Gold			12 yds. [11m]

Worsted-weight	Nylon Plus™	Need-loft®	YARN AMOUNT
☐ Holly	#31	#27	2½ oz. [70.9g]
☐ Red	#20	#01	54 yds. [49.4m]

STITCH KEY:
- French Knot

C – Ornament Side
(cut 2) 22 x 25 holes

A – Wall Motif Front & Backing
(cut 1 each) 73 x 87 holes

Fireside Comforts For The Family

Lasting Memories
for your
Best Friend

Chapter Two

FROSTY PHOTO FUN

Designed by
Vicki Staggs

Gift Idea

Put in successive pictures of you and your friend over a span of years to see how you two have changed, but not grown apart over the years. Send updated photos each year thereafter. A gift of this smiling man of snow will convey a message of warmth by saying, "Thanks for being my friend!"

SIZE: 8¾" x 14¾" [22.2cm x 37.5cm], with four 1"-square [2.5cm] photo windows.

MATERIALS: Two sheets of 7-count plastic canvas; Two 18" [45.7cm] lengths of 20-gauge floral wire; Two navy ¾" [1.9cm] shank buttons; White craft paint; Four 1" [2.5cm] photos; Pencil; Craft glue or glue gun; Worsted-weight or plastic canvas yarn (for amounts see Color Key).

CUTTING INSTRUCTIONS:

NOTE: Graphs continued on page 34.
A: For Snowman front and backing, cut two (one for front and one for backing) according to graph.
B: For arms #1 and #2, cut one each according to graphs.
C: For feet #1 and #2, cut one each according to graphs.
D: For scarf pieces #1 and #2, cut one each according to graphs.
E: For frames, cut four according to graph.

STITCHING INSTRUCTIONS:

NOTE: Backing A is not worked.
1: Using colors and stitches indicated, work one A for front and D pieces according to graphs; fill in uncoded areas of front A and work B and C pieces using eggshell and Continental Stitch. With royal dark for scarf pieces and with matching colors, Overcast edges of B-D pieces; with burgundy, forest, pumpkin and royal dark, Overcast edges of one E piece in each color.
2: Using burgundy and embroidery stitches indicated, embroider mouth on front A as indicated on graph.
3: Holding backing A to wrong side of front A, with matching colors, Whipstitch together.
NOTE: Cut one 14" [35.6cm], two 10" [25.4cm] and one 2" [5.1cm] piece of wire.
4: For hand connector, thread one end of 14" wire from back to front through ✦ hole on each B piece as indicated; wrap ends tightly around pencil to curl and slide wire off pencil.
5: For each foot connector, thread ends of one 10" wire through one C and corresponding ✦ hole on A as indicated (see photo); curl wire as for hand connector in Step 4, and twist wire ends to secure.
NOTE: Cut one 18" [45.7cm] length of pumpkin.
6: For nose, thread ends of 2" wire from front to back through ▲ hole on snowman and twist together on wrong side to secure; assemble wire and pumpkin strand according to Nose Assembly Diagram on page 34.
7: For each eye, cut shank off one button. Paint a starburst on each button as shown; let dry. Glue eyes to face as indicated.
8: Glue arms and scarf pieces to Snowman as shown. Glue photos to wrong sides of frames and frames to hand connector as shown. Hang or display as desired.✢

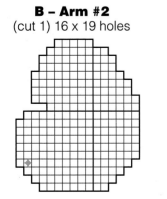

B – Arm #2
(cut 1) 16 x 19 holes

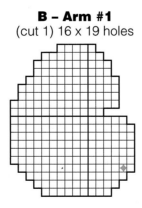

B – Arm #1
(cut 1) 16 x 19 holes

COLOR KEY: Frosty Photo Fun

Worsted-weight	Nylon Plus™	Need-loft®	YARN AMOUNT
☐ Eggshell	#24	#39	52 yds. [47.5m]
■ Royal Dark	#07	#48	15 yds. [13.7m]
■ Burgundy	#13	#03	5 yds. [4.6m]
▨ Pumpkin	#50	#12	4½ yds. [4.2m]
▨ Forest	#32	#29	4 yds. [3.7m]

STITCH KEY:
— Backstitch/Straight
✦ Connector Attachment
▲ Nose Attachment
○ Eye Placement

FROSTY PHOTO FUN

(Instructions & photo on pages 32 & 33.)

E – Frame
(cut 4)
9 x 9 holes

Cut
Out

C – Foot #1
(cut 1) 18 x 21 holes

D – Scarf Piece #1
(cut 1) 14 x 14 holes

D – Scarf Piece #2
(cut 1) 12 x 14 holes

A – Snowman Front & Backing
(cut 1 each) 44 x 75 holes

C – Foot #2
(cut 1) 18 x 21 holes

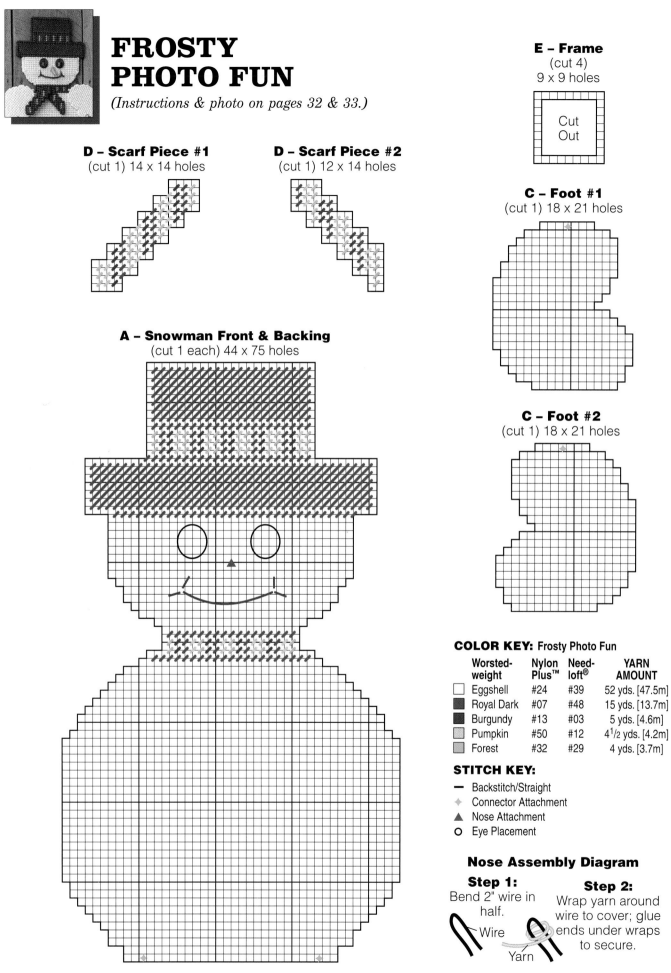

COLOR KEY: Frosty Photo Fun

Worsted-weight	Nylon Plus™	Need-loft®	YARN AMOUNT
☐ Eggshell	#24	#39	52 yds. [47.5m]
■ Royal Dark	#07	#48	15 yds. [13.7m]
■ Burgundy	#13	#03	5 yds. [4.6m]
☐ Pumpkin	#50	#12	4½ yds. [4.2m]
☐ Forest	#32	#29	4 yds. [3.7m]

STITCH KEY:
— Backstitch/Straight
✦ Connector Attachment
▲ Nose Attachment
○ Eye Placement

Nose Assembly Diagram

Step 1:
Bend 2" wire in half.
Wire

Step 2:
Wrap yarn around wire to cover; glue ends under wraps to secure.
Yarn

WEDDING DREAMS

Designed by Carol Nartowicz

Instructions on next page

Gift Idea

Surprise the happy couple with a video vignette of a special occasion, like the ceremony or reception, using this beautiful wedding case as the gift box for the tape. Be sure to include a special snapshot in the photo pocket.

35

WEDDING DREAMS

(Photo on page 35.)

SIZE: 1⅝" x 4¾" x 8¼" [4.1cm x 12.1cm x 21cm], with a 2¼" x 3" [5.7cm x 7.6cm] photo window.

MATERIALS: 1½ sheets of 7-count plastic canvas; Two clear 4" [10.2cm] squares of heavy vinyl; Sewing needle and white thread; ⅓ yd. [0.3m] white ¼" [6mm] picot-edged satin ribbon; ⅓ yd. [0.3m] white ⅜" [10mm] eyelet trim; Two silver ¾" [19mm] novelty wedding rings; Craft glue or glue gun; Metallic cord (for amount see Color Key); Worsted-weight or plastic canvas yarn (for amount see Color Key).

CUTTING INSTRUCTIONS:

A: For cover, cut one according to graph.

B: For cover sides, cut two 8 x 53 holes.
C: For cover ends, cut two 8 x 30 holes.
D: For tray, cut one 29 x 51 holes.
E: For tray side, cut one 7 x 51 holes (no graph).
F: For tray ends, cut two 7 x 29 holes (no graph).
G: For heart pieces, cut ten according to graph.

STITCHING INSTRUCTIONS:

NOTE: E, F and eight G pieces are not worked.
1: Using colors and stitches indicated, work A-D and two G pieces according to graphs; with white, Overcast cutout edges of A.
2: For each heart, holding four unworked G pieces to wrong side of one worked G, with white, Whipstitch together through all thicknesses.
3: With white, Whipstitch A-F pieces together according to Wedding Dreams Assembly Diagram.
4: With sewing needle and thread, tack

A – Cover
(cut 1) 30 x 53 holes

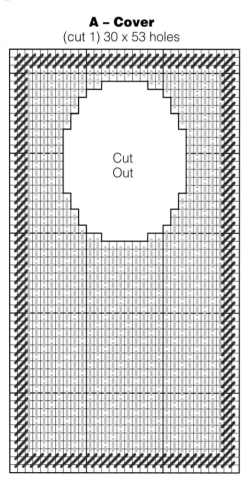

Cut Out

B – Cover Side
(cut 2)
8 x 53 holes

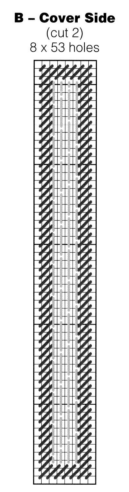

G – Heart Piece
(cut 10)
11 x 11 holes

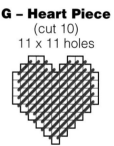

C – Cover End
(cut 2)
8 x 30 holes

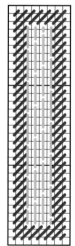

Lasting Memories For Your Best Friend

both vinyl pieces to wrong side of cover over cutout, leaving bottom edges open for photo.

5: Slip ribbon through rings and tie into a small bow; trim ends. Glue hearts and bow to cover; glue trim around cutout as shown in photo, trimming away excess as needed.‡

D – Tray
(cut 1) 29 x 51 holes

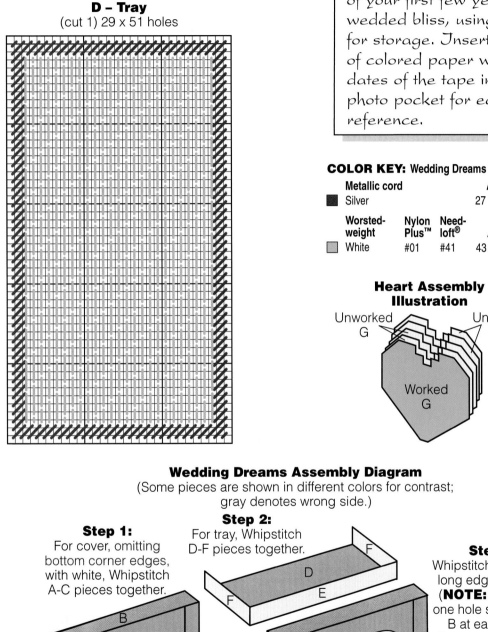

Tip

You can also use the wedding case for videos of anniversary parties. Or, make a special tape of each of your first few years of wedded bliss, using the case for storage. Insert a piece of colored paper with the dates of the tape in the photo pocket for easy reference.

COLOR KEY: Wedding Dreams

			AMOUNT
Metallic cord			
■ Silver			27 yds. [24.7m]

	Worsted-weight	Nylon Plus™	Need-loft®	YARN AMOUNT
☐	White	#01	#41	43 yds. [39.3m]

Heart Assembly Illustration

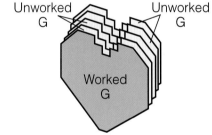

Unworked G   Unworked G

Worked G

Wedding Dreams Assembly Diagram
(Some pieces are shown in different colors for contrast; gray denotes wrong side.)

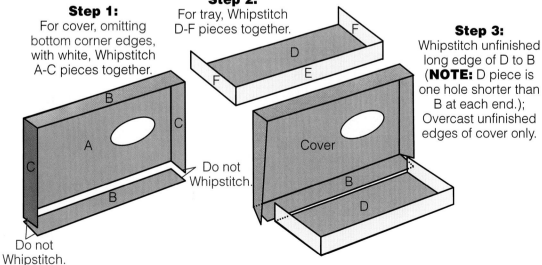

Step 1:
For cover, omitting bottom corner edges, with white, Whipstitch A-C pieces together.

B
C
A
C
B
Do not Whipstitch.
Do not Whipstitch.

Step 2:
For tray, Whipstitch D-F pieces together.

F
D
F
E

Step 3:
Whipstitch unfinished long edge of D to B (**NOTE:** D piece is one hole shorter than B at each end.); Overcast unfinished edges of cover only.

Cover
B
D

Lasting Memories For Your Best Friend

SIZE: 3¾" x 9¾" x 9¾" tall [9.5cm x 24.8cm x 24.8cm], not including handles.

MATERIALS: Three sheets of 7-count plastic canvas; Four black ¾" [19mm] buttons; #5 pearl cotton or six-strand embroidery floss (for amount see Color Key); Worsted-weight or plastic canvas yarn (for amounts see Color Key).

CUTTING INSTRUCTIONS:

NOTE: Graphs continued on pages 40 & 41.

A: For front, cut one 64 x 64 holes.

B: For back, cut one 64 x 64 holes.

C: For sides and bottom, cut three (two for sides and one for bottom) 25 x 64 holes.

D: For handles, cut two 5 x 89 holes (no graph).

STITCHING INSTRUCTIONS:

1: Using colors and stitches indicated, work A-C and one D piece according to graphs and stitch pattern guide; fill in uncoded areas of A using straw and Continental Stitch. Substituting Xmas red for Xmas green, work remaining D piece according to stitch pattern guide. With Xmas red for Xmas green handle and Xmas green for Xmas red handle, Overcast edges of D pieces.

2: Using pearl cotton or three strands floss and embroidery stitches indicated, embroider detail on A and B pieces as indicated on graphs.

3: Whipstitch and assemble pieces as indicated and according to Tote Assembly Diagram.✢

Tote Assembly Diagram
(Gray denotes wrong side.)

Step 1:
With Xmas red, Whipstitch A-C pieces together; Overcast unfinished edges.

Side C

B

Side C

A

Bottom C

Step 2:
To attach each handle end, holding D to right side of front or back, with pearl cotton or floss, sew one button to Tote through all thicknesses.

D

Button

COLOR KEY: Waiting for Santa

Pearl cotton or floss			AMOUNT
Black			8 yds. [7.3m]

Worsted-weight	Nylon Plus™	Need-loft®	YARN AMOUNT
Xmas Red	#19	#02	90 yds. [82.3m]
Xmas Green	#58	#28	80 yds. [73.2m]
White	#01	#41	24 yds. [22m]
Straw	#41	#19	22 yds. [20.1m]
Rust	#51	#09	11 yds. [10.1m]
Gold	#27	#17	8 yds. [7.3m]
Gray	#23	#38	8 yds. [7.3m]
Cinnamon	#44	#14	7 yds. [6.4m]
Black	#02	#00	3 yds. [2.7m]
Pumpkin	#50	#12	2 yds. [1.8m]
Silver	–	#37	2 yds. [1.8m]
Tangerine	#15	#11	2 yds. [1.8m]
Yellow	#26	#57	2 yds. [1.8m]
Coral	#14	#66	½ yd. [0.5m]

STITCH KEY:
- — Backstitch/Straight
- • French Knot
- □ Handle Attachment

C – Side & Bottom
(cut 3) 25 x 64 holes

WAITING FOR SANTA

(Instructions & photo on pages 38 & 39.)

Gift Idea

Being a giving person is one of the chief joys in life, so present someone you know with this hearthside bag filled with new needles or hooks, a special threader, new cutters, a color wheel or chart, or even some new patterns for your friend's favorite craft.

Handle Stitch Pattern Guide

Continue established pattern across each entire piece.

COLOR KEY: Waiting for Santa

	Pearl cotton or floss			AMOUNT
■	Black			8 yds. [7.3m]

	Worsted-weight	Nylon Plus™	Need-loft®	YARN AMOUNT
■	Xmas Red	#19	#02	90 yds. [82.3m]
■	Xmas Green	#58	#28	80 yds. [73.2m]
▨	White	#01	#41	24 yds. [22m]
□	Straw	#41	#19	22 yds. [20.1m]
■	Rust	#51	#09	11 yds. [10.1m]
▨	Gold	#27	#17	8 yds. [7.3m]
■	Gray	#23	#38	8 yds. [7.3m]
■	Cinnamon	#44	#14	7 yds. [6.4m]
■	Black	#02	#00	3 yds. [2.7m]
■	Pumpkin	#50	#12	2 yds. [1.8m]
■	Silver	–	#37	2 yds. [1.8m]
■	Tangerine	#15	#11	2 yds. [1.8m]
▨	Yellow	#26	#57	2 yds. [1.8m]
□	Coral	#14	#66	¹/₂ yd. [0.5m]

STITCH KEY:

— Backstitch/Straight
• French Knot
□ Handle Attachment

A – Front (cut 1) 64 x 64 holes

Lasting Memories For Your Best Friend

B – Back (cut 1) 64 x 64 holes

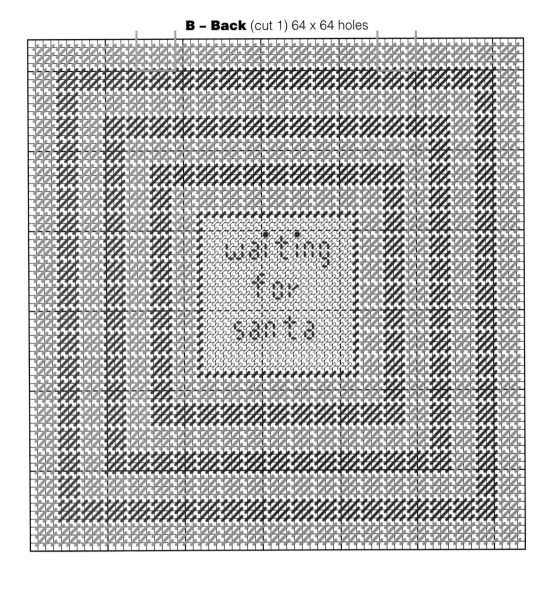

Heartwarming Story

Grandparents are very special people, and they can bridge generations with the wonderful stories they tell. Often, on cold winter days, we would visit my grandparents and gather around the fireplace to listen to my grandfather's stories of his youth. We were excited and inspired by his tales, but we also learned lessons by identifying with and understanding the actions and consequences Granddad faced. We soon discovered that we could learn from others and that if we just listen, we can choose our paths in life more wisely, carefully and with less pain. — Kim Votaw

SEW SALLY

Designed by Janelle Giese of Janelle Marie Designs

SIZE: 8¾" across x about 9½" tall [22.2cm x 24.1cm].

MATERIALS: Four sheets of 7-count plastic canvas; ½ sheet of 10-count plastic canvas; One package of blonde wool doll hair; 4"-square [10.2cm] scrap of desired-color fabric; Polyester fiberfill; Craft glue or glue gun; #3 pearl cotton (for amounts see Color Key on page 44); Six-strand embroidery floss (for amounts see Color Key); ⅛" [3mm] metallic ribbon or heavy metallic braid (for amounts see Color Key); Worsted-weight or plastic canvas yarn (for amount see Color Key).

CUTTING INSTRUCTIONS:

NOTES: Use 10-count for N and O pieces and 7-count canvas for remaining pieces. Graphs on pages 44-47.

A: For base, cut one according to graph.

B: For skirt wide panels, cut four according to graph.

C: For skirt narrow panels, cut four according to graph.

D: For skirt wide pockets, cut four 10 x 30 holes.

E: For skirt narrow pockets, cut four 10 x 29 holes.

F: For apron cap, cut one according to graph.

G: For apron inserts, cut four according to graph.

H: For apron bodice, cut one according to graph.

I: For sleeve caps #1 and #2, cut one each according to graphs.

J: For arms #1 and #2, cut one each according to graphs.

K: For collar, cut one 2 x 19 holes (no graph).

L: For basket side, cut one according to graph.

M: For basket bottom, cut one according to graph.

N: For head front, cut one according to graph.

O: For head back, cut one according to graph.

STITCHING INSTRUCTIONS:

NOTE: A piece is not worked.

1: Using colors and stitches indicated, work B-G, H (fold in half, overlap at each end as indicated on graph and work through both thicknesses at overlap areas to join), I, J, L (overlap ends as indicated and work through both thicknesses at overlap area to join) and M pieces according to graphs. Fill in un-

Heartwarming Story

In elementary school, I had a special friend who would always give me small tokens of friendship. Some things she gave me were useless to everyone else, but they meant a lot to me because they were given from the heart. Such things that passed between us were anything from snails to friendship beads, but they all stood for comradeship. We continued this up into high school, more as a joke than anything else. It's so nice to share memories in that way with a close friend. Even after we moved apart, we would send small things like stickers and comic strips in our letters. These little gifts have kept us in touch in a special way all these years. Storing these treasures is like saving up memories that I'll never want to lose. — Kim Votaw

SEW SALLY

(Continued from page 43.)

coded areas of J pieces on opposite side of canvas and work K (overlap ends four holes and work through both thicknesses at overlap area to join) using white and Continental Stitch.

2: Using metallic ribbon or braid in colors indicated and Straight Stitch, embroider detail on D and E pieces as indicated.

3: Whipstitch A-E pieces together as indicated and according to Base Assembly Diagram; Whipstitch F-H and K pieces together as indicated and according to Apron Assembly Diagram on page 47.

4: For each sleeve, Whipstitch one of each corresponding I and J piece together and to apron as indicated and according to Sleeve Assembly Diagram.

5: With camel, Whipstitch X edges of L wrong sides together; Whipstitch L and M pieces together and Overcast unfinished top edge, forming basket. For pincushion, place a small ball of fiberfill in center of fabric square; fold over ends of fabric to cover fiberfill, then glue ends inside basket to secure. Glue, or with coral, tack basket to hands as shown in photo.

6: For head, using pearl cotton and six strands floss in colors indicated and Continental Stitch, work N and O pieces according to graphs.

7: Using four strands dk. coffee brown floss and Straight Stitch, embroider eyes (work two stitches for each eye), eyelashes, nose and mouth on N as indicated; using one strand terra cotta floss and Cross Stitch, embroider cheeks as indicated. Using one strand med. dk. shell pink and Backstitch, embroider cheek and lip outlines as indicated.

8: For each dart, with matching colors,

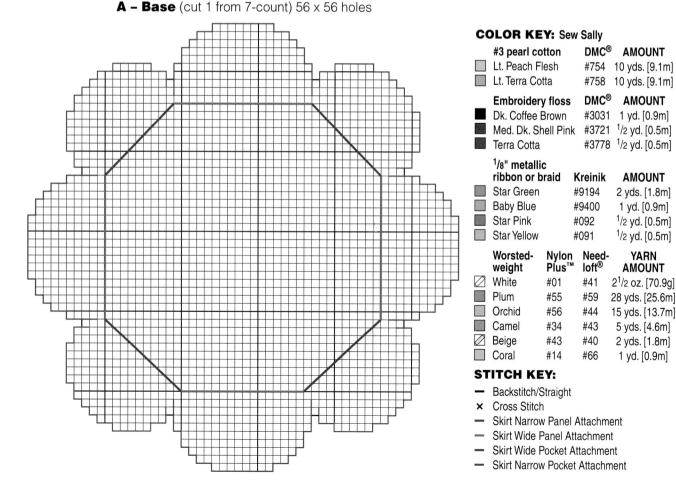

A – Base (cut 1 from 7-count) 56 x 56 holes

COLOR KEY: Sew Sally

#3 pearl cotton	DMC®	AMOUNT
Lt. Peach Flesh	#754	10 yds. [9.1m]
Lt. Terra Cotta	#758	10 yds. [9.1m]

Embroidery floss	DMC®	AMOUNT
Dk. Coffee Brown	#3031	1 yd. [0.9m]
Med. Dk. Shell Pink	#3721	1/2 yd. [0.5m]
Terra Cotta	#3778	1/2 yd. [0.5m]

1/8" metallic ribbon or braid	Kreinik	AMOUNT
Star Green	#9194	2 yds. [1.8m]
Baby Blue	#9400	1 yd. [0.9m]
Star Pink	#092	1/2 yd. [0.5m]
Star Yellow	#091	1/2 yd. [0.5m]

Worsted-weight	Nylon Plus™	Need-loft®	YARN AMOUNT
White	#01	#41	2 1/2 oz. [70.9g]
Plum	#55	#59	28 yds. [25.6m]
Orchid	#56	#44	15 yds. [13.7m]
Camel	#34	#43	5 yds. [4.6m]
Beige	#43	#40	2 yds. [1.8m]
Coral	#14	#66	1 yd. [0.9m]

STITCH KEY:

- — Backstitch/Straight
- × Cross Stitch
- — Skirt Narrow Panel Attachment
- — Skirt Wide Panel Attachment
- — Skirt Wide Pocket Attachment
- — Skirt Narrow Pocket Attachment

Whipstitch X and Y edges on each N and O piece wrong sides together as indicated. Whipstitch N and O pieces wrong sides together according to Head Assembly Illustration; Overcast unfinished edges.

9: Curving neck of head to fit, glue neck inside collar on apron (see photo). Glue hair to head as desired. Aligning apron inserts over narrow skirt panels, place apron over base skirt (see photo).✝

D – Skirt Wide Pocket
(cut 4 from 7-count) 10 x 30 holes

— Whipstitch to A. —

E – Skirt Narrow Pocket
(cut 4 from 7-count) 10 x 29 holes

— Whipstitch to A. —

B – Skirt Wide Panel
(cut 4 from 7-count)
17 x 24 holes

└ Whipstitch to A. ┘

C – Skirt Narrow Panel
(cut 4 from 7-count)
13 x 24 holes

Whipstitch to A.

Base Assembly Diagram
(Pieces are shown in different colors for contrast; gray denotes wrong side.)

Step 1:
With white, Whipstitch A-C pieces together; Overcast unfinished edges of B and C pieces.

F – Apron Cap (cut 1 from 7-count) 40 x 40 holes

Whipstitch to one G between arrows.

Whipstitch to one G between arrows.

Whipstitch to one G between arrows.

Cut Out

Whipstitch to one G between arrows.

Whipstitch to one G between arrows.

Step 2:
Alternating panels, Whipstitch short ends of D and E pieces right sides together.

Step 3:
With plum, Whipstitch D and E pieces to A; Overcast unfinished edges.

Step 4:
With white, tack upper corners of D and E pieces to skirt panel seams.

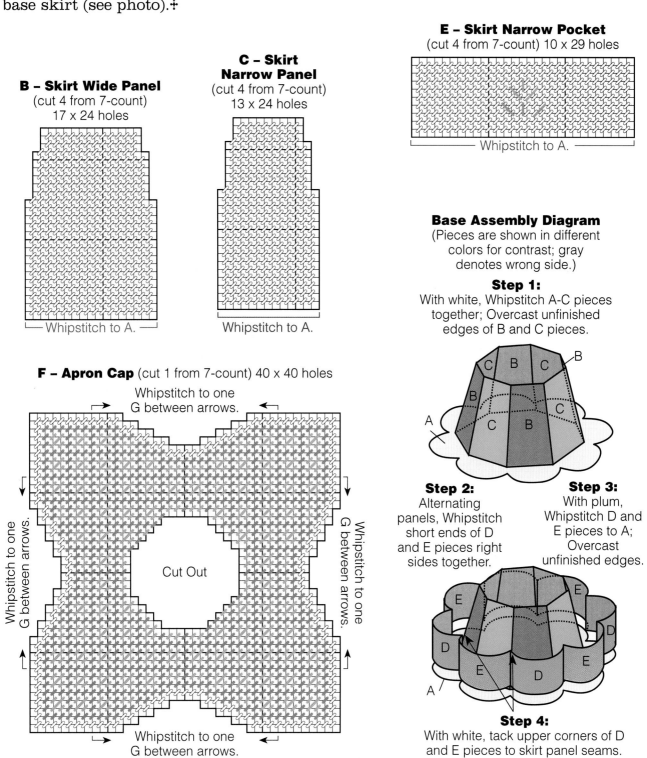

SEW SALLY

(Instructions & photo on pages 42 & 43.)

H – Apron Bodice
(cut 1 from 7-count) 24 x 33 holes

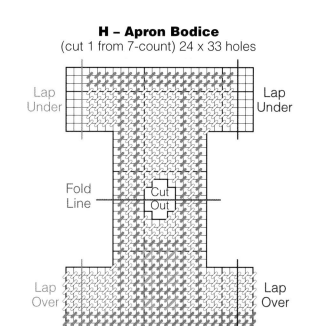

Lap Under

Lap Under

Fold Line

Cut Out

Lap Over

Lap Over

COLOR KEY: Sew Sally

#3 pearl cotton		DMC®	AMOUNT
	Lt. Peach Flesh	#754	10 yds. [9.1m]
	Lt. Terra Cotta	#758	10 yds. [9.1m]

Embroidery floss		DMC®	AMOUNT
	Dk. Coffee Brown	#3031	1 yd. [0.9m]
	Med. Dk. Shell Pink	#3721	$1/2$ yd. [0.5m]
	Terra Cotta	#3778	$1/2$ yd. [0.5m]

1/8" metallic ribbon or braid		Kreinik	AMOUNT
	Star Green	#9194	2 yds. [1.8m]
	Baby Blue	#9400	1 yd. [0.9m]
	Star Pink	#092	$1/2$ yd. [0.5m]
	Star Yellow	#091	$1/2$ yd. [0.5m]

Worsted-weight	Nylon Plus™	Need-loft®	YARN AMOUNT
White	#01	#41	$2 1/2$ oz. [70.9g]
Plum	#55	#59	28 yds. [25.6m]
Orchid	#56	#44	15 yds. [13.7m]
Camel	#34	#43	5 yds. [4.6m]
Beige	#43	#40	2 yds. [1.8m]
Coral	#14	#66	1 yd. [0.9m]

STITCH KEY:

- Backstitch/Straight
× Cross Stitch
- Skirt Narrow Panel Attachment
- Skirt Wide Panel Attachment
- Skirt Wide Pocket Attachment
- Skirt Narrow Pocket Attachment

G – Apron Insert
(cut 4 from 7-count) 12 x 12 holes

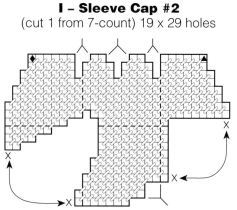

Whipstitch to F between arrows.

I – Sleeve Cap #1
(cut 1 from 7-count) 19 x 29 holes

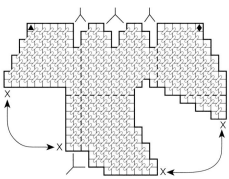

Whipstitch X and Y edges together.

I – Sleeve Cap #2
(cut 1 from 7-count) 19 x 29 holes

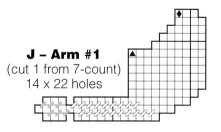

Whipstitch X and Y edges together.

J – Arm #2
(cut 1 from 7-count) 14 x 22 holes

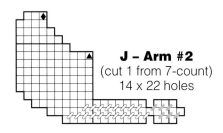

J – Arm #1
(cut 1 from 7-count) 14 x 22 holes

N – Head Front

(cut 1 from 10-count) 28 x 30 holes
Whipstitch X and Y edges together.

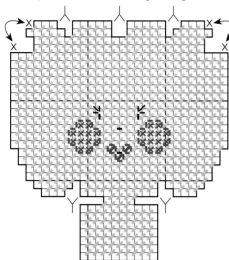

L – Basket Side

(cut 1 from 7-count) 7 x 36 holes

Lap Over

Lap Under

Whipstitch Y edges together.

O – Head Back

(cut 1 from 10-count) 24 x 30 holes
Whipstitch X and Y edges together.

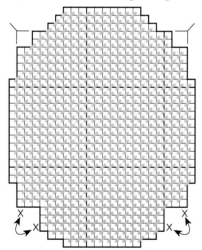

Sleeve Assembly Diagram

(Pieces are shown in different colors
for contrast; gray denotes wrong side.)

Step 1:
With white, Whipstitch each X,
then each Y edge of one I wrong
sides together, forming darts.

Step 3:
With matching
colors, Overcast
unfinished edges of
arm and hand.

Sleeve/Arm
#2

I#2

J#2

H

Overlap

Overlap

Step 4:
With white,
Whipstitch sleeve
to corresponding
opening on H.

Step 2:
Matching ♦ and ▲ symbols,
Whipstitch I and corresponding
J piece wrong sides together.

Apron Assembly Diagram

(Pieces are shown in different colors for contrast; gray denotes wrong side.)

Step 1:
With white, Whipstitch K to
small cutout on H; Overcast
unfinished edges of K.

K

Overlap

Overlap

H

F

Step 2:
Facing bib (bodice front) to
one cap point, with plum,
Whipstitch H to cutout on
right side of F.

G

G

G

F

G

Step 3:
(Bodice not shown.)
Bending points of cap downward,
Whipstitch F and G pieces together;
with matching colors, Overcast
unfinished edges.

M – Basket Bottom

(cut 1 from
7-count)
8 x 8 holes

Head Assembly Illustration

(back view)

N

O

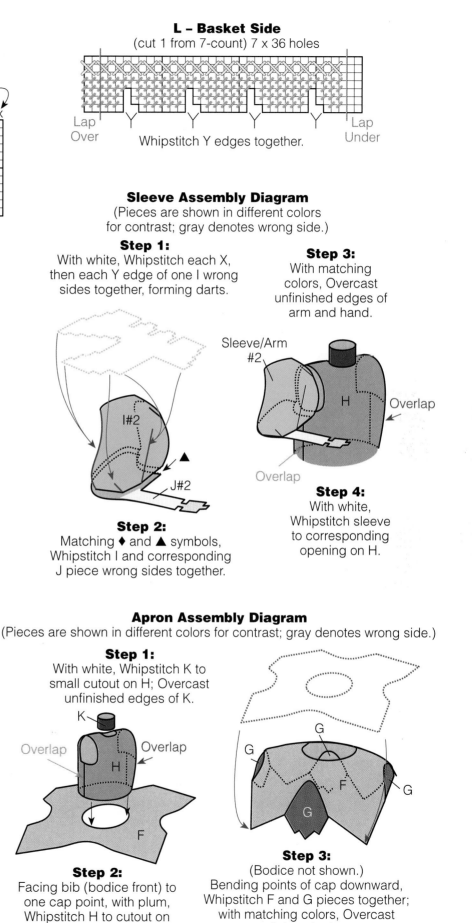

WINTER GIFT BOX

Designed by
Michele Wilcox

Gift Idea

This uplifting box, featuring an icy friend standing guard in the elements, is perfect for providing those cold weather "necessities" for someone you love. Why not treat someone special to their very own winter survival kit with this frosty sentinel as the cheerful messenger? Try putting in all those things you just can't live without in the still of winter, such as lip balm, hot drink packets, candy bars, popcorn, a fun mug or even a phone card. Then this smiling snowman will be happy to deliver.

SIZE: 6⅜" x 7½" x 4" tall [16.2cm x 19cm x 10.2cm].

MATERIALS: Two sheets of 7-count plastic canvas; #3 pearl cotton or six-strand embroidery floss (for amount see Color Key); Worsted-weight or plastic canvas yarn (for amounts see Color Key).

CUTTING INSTRUCTIONS:

A: For lid top, cut one 41 x 49 holes.

B: For lid sides, cut two 8 x 49 holes (no graph).

C: For lid ends, cut two 8 x 41 holes (no graph).

D: For box bottom, cut one 39 x 47 holes.

E: For box sides, cut two 24 x 47 holes (no graph).

F: For box ends, cut two 24 x 39 holes (no graph).

STITCHING INSTRUCTIONS:

1: Using colors and stitches indicated, work pieces according to graphs and stitch pattern guide on page 50.

2: Using pearl cotton or six strands floss and embroidery stitches indicated, embroider detail on A piece as indicated on graph.

3: With eggshell, Whipstitch pieces together according to Winter Gift Box Assembly Illustration on page 50; Overcast unfinished edges.✛

COLOR KEY: Winter Gift Box

Pearl cotton or floss			AMOUNT
■ Black			2 yds. [1.8m]

Worsted-weight	Nylon Plus™	Need-loft®	YARN AMOUNT
▨ Rose	#52	#06	3 oz. [85.1g]
▧ Eggshell	#24	#39	66 yds. [60.4m]
■ Royal Dark	#07	#48	9 yds. [8.2m]
▨ Holly	#31	#27	7 yds. [6.4m]
▨ Mermaid Green	#37	#53	7 yds. [6.4m]
▨ Cinnamon	#44	#14	1 yd. [0.9m]
■ Coral	#14	#66	½ yd. [0.5m]

STITCH KEY:

— Backstitch/Straight

● French Knot

A – Lid Top
(cut 1) 41 x 49 holes

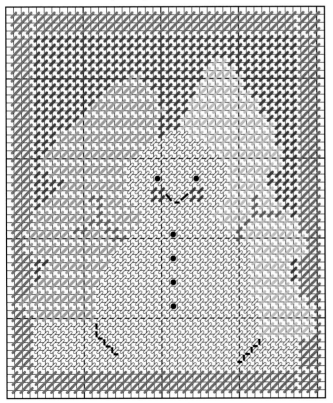

D – Box Bottom
(cut 1) 39 x 47 holes

WINTER GIFT BOX

(Instructions & photo on pages 48 & 49.)

COLOR KEY: Winter Gift Box

Pearl cotton or floss			AMOUNT
■ Black			2 yds. [1.8m]

Worsted-weight	Nylon Plus™	Need-loft®	YARN AMOUNT
■ Rose	#52	#06	3 oz. [85.1g]
▨ Eggshell	#24	#39	66 yds. [60.4m]
■ Royal Dark	#07	#48	9 yds. [8.2m]
□ Holly	#31	#27	7 yds. [6.4m]
□ Mermaid Green	#37	#53	7 yds. [6.4m]
■ Cinnamon	#44	#14	1 yd. [0.9m]
■ Coral	#14	#66	¹/₂ yd. [0.5m]

STITCH KEY:

− Backstitch/Straight
● French Knot

Side & End Stitch Pattern Guide

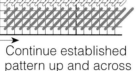

Continue established pattern up and across each entire piece.

Winter Gift Box Assembly Illustration

(Pieces are shown in different colors for contrast; gray denotes wrong side.)

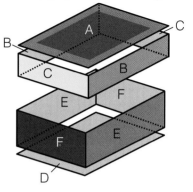

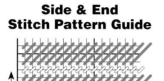

Heartwarming Story

Several years ago, my brother and I made a three-week trip to Colorado for two friends' wedding. While there, one of the groomsmen decided to go skiing. The whole town was abuzz when he didn't come back that night, or the next day. Our minds quickly thought the worst — a skiing accident. We've all heard stories of frightening circumstances where people are stranded in frigid climates, and they are tested in survival skills. Two days later, after rescuers were looking for our lost companion, the tardy one showed up at the bride's house. He soon set the record straight and told everyone he never even made it to the ski resort because his vehicle broke down and he had to catch a ride to a service station, and back again to the stranded automobile. He related some frightening incidents that nearly cost him his life (he was nearly run over several times and robbed), and we couldn't help but be relieved that he made it back alive. Only with the help of an elderly man was he even able to repair his vehicle so that he could return to his anxious friends. We realized then and there that survival skills were necessary for more than just battles with nature, and that perfect strangers can sometimes be our guardian angels. — Kim Votaw

MAY FLOWER MEDLEY

Designed by Patricia Hall

Instructions on next page

MAY FLOWER MEDLEY

(Photo on page 51.)

SIZES: Tissue Cover snugly covers a boutique-style tissue box; Frame is 6⅛" x 7½" [15.6cm x 19cm] with a 3¾" x 5⅛" [9.5cm x 13cm] photo window; Coaster Holder is 5" x 5" x 1¾" tall [12.7cm x 12.7cm x 4.4cm]; each Coaster is 4⅛" square [10.5cm].

MATERIALS: Two sheets of clear and three sheets of white 7-count plastic canvas; 5" x 7" [12.7cm x 17.8cm] clear acrylic frame; Craft glue or glue gun; Worsted-weight or plastic canvas yarn (for amounts see Color Key).

CUTTING INSTRUCTIONS:
NOTE: Use clear for A-D and white canvas for remaining pieces.
A: For Tissue Cover sides, cut four 31 x 37 holes.
B: For Tissue Cover top, cut one according to graph.
C: For flowers, cut fifteen according to graph.
D: For leaves, cut thirty-seven according to graph.
E: For Frame front and backing, cut two (one for front and one for backing) according to graph.
F: For Coaster Holder bottom, cut one from white 31 x 31 holes (no graph).
G: For Coaster Holder sides and linings, cut eight 10 x 13 holes for sides and eight 10 x 12 holes for linings (no lining graph).
H: For Coasters, cut six according to graph.

STITCHING INSTRUCTIONS:
NOTE: Backing E, F and lining G pieces are not worked.
1: Using colors and stitches indicated, work A, B, six C, D, one E for front, side G and H pieces according to graphs; substituting pink and lavender for sail blue, work five C pieces in pink and four in lavender according to graph.
2: With yellow for flower centers and with matching colors, Overcast cutout edges of B and edges of C and D pieces.
3: With white, Whipstitch A and B pieces together, forming Tissue Cover; Overcast unfinished bottom edges.
4: For Frame, holding backing E to wrong side of front E, with white, Whipstitch together; center and glue to acrylic frame.
5: Whipstitch F and G pieces together according to Coaster Holder Assembly Diagram.
6: Glue flowers and leaves to Tissue Cover, Frame and Coaster Holder as desired or as shown in photo.✝

C – Flower
(cut 15 from clear)
7 x 7 holes

D – Leaf
(cut 37 from clear)
5 x 8 holes

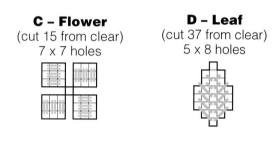

Gift Idea

A gift of this set will be like sending a box of fresh-picked flowers. Of course, your friend would appreciate it even more if you sent along a photo of the two of you together, enjoying those ice cream cones, modeling your newly-bought outfits or embracing at each other's weddings. Then, wrap the gift box with floral paper and use a beautiful blooming rose, carnations or mums for a spectacular package topper.

E – Frame Front & Backing
(cut 1 each from white)
40 x 49 holes

Cut Out

A – Tissue Cover Side
(cut 4 from clear) 31 x 37 holes

B – Tissue Cover Top
(cut 1 from clear) 31 x 31 holes

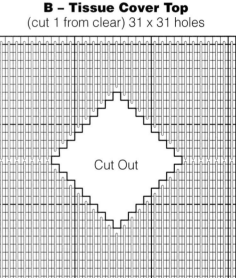

Cut Out

COLOR KEY: May Flower Medley

	Worsted-weight	Nylon Plus™	Need-loft®	YARN AMOUNT
▨	White	#01	#41	70 yds. [64m]
▨	Lime	#29	#22	38 yds. [34.7m]
■	Lavender	#12	#05	17 yds. [15.5m]
▨	Pink	#11	#07	14 yds. [12.8m]
▨	Sail Blue	#04	#35	8 yds. [7.3m]
☐	Yellow	#26	#57	3 yds. [2.7m]

G – Coaster Holder Side
(cut 8 from white)
10 x 13 holes

H – Coaster
(cut 6 from white) 27 x 27 holes

Cut out gray areas and
around blue bars carefully.

Coaster Holder Assembly Diagram
(Pieces are shown in different colors for contrast.)

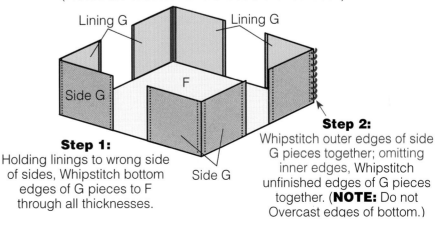

Lining G   Lining G

Side G   F

Side G

Step 1:
Holding linings to wrong side
of sides, Whipstitch bottom
edges of G pieces to F
through all thicknesses.

Step 2:
Whipstitch outer edges of side
G pieces together; omitting
inner edges, Whipstitch
unfinished edges of G pieces
together. (**NOTE:** Do not
Overcast edges of bottom.)

Loving Touches
for the
Romantics

Chapter Three

LACE & ROSES BATH

Designed by Sandra Miller Maxfield

Instructions on pages 58 & 59

Gift Idea

For a lovely gift set, put a nice set of silver brushes, combs and hair clips in the planter. In the heart basket, place a pocket-sized book of poetry, a cassette or compact disc of peaceful nature sounds and a box of scented bath salts. Then, tie a shimmery ribbon around both of them and present them to a friend. Your reward will be the look of anticipated relaxation coming across your friend's face.

LACE & ROSES BATH

(Photo on pages 56 & 57.)

SIZES: Wall Basket is 4" x 8¼" x 7¼" tall [10.2cm x 21cm x 18.4cm]; Tissue Cover is 5½" x 10¼" x 3¼" tall [14cm x 26cm x 8.3cm]; Planter is 4⅜" across x 4¾" tall [11.1cm x 12.1cm]. Measurements do not include lace, trim or flowers.

MATERIALS: Five sheets of 7-count plastic canvas; ½ sheet of 12" x 18" [30.5cm x 45.7cm] or larger 7-count plastic canvas (for Planter); Darice® 4¼" [10.8cm] half-radial circle, Standard-size washcloth, hand towel and bath towel; 3¼ yds. [3m] each of gold ½" [13mm] scallop-edged trim, mauve 2" [5.1cm] crochet-edged lace and forest 1¼" [3.2cm] lace; 100-count package of 3mm gold beads; Assorted artificial flowers of choice; Nine burgundy ⅝" [16mm] satin ribbon rosebuds with leaves; Sewing needle and gold thread; Craft glue or glue gun; Worsted-weight or plastic canvas yarn (for amounts see Color Key).

CUTTING INSTRUCTIONS:

NOTE: Graphs continued on page 60.

A: For Wall Basket front and back, cut two (one for front and one for back) according to graph.

B: For Wall Basket sides, cut two 26 x 63 holes (no graph).

C: For Wall Basket heart motif, cut one according to graph.

D: For Wall Basket hanger, cut one according to graph.

E: For Tissue Cover sides, cut two 21 x 67 holes (no graph).

F: For Tissue Cover ends, cut two 21 x 35 holes (no graph).

G: For Tissue Cover top, cut one according to graph.

H: For Planter side, cut one 31 x 84 holes.

I: For Planter bottom, cut away one outer row of holes from 4¼" circle (no graph).

J: For Planter rim, cut one 11 x 94 holes (no graph).

STITCHING INSTRUCTIONS:

NOTE: Back A, D and I pieces are not worked.

1: Using colors and stitches indicated, work one A for front, C, G and H pieces according to graphs and B, E, F and J (Overlap ends as indicated on guide and work through both thicknesses at overlap area to join.) pieces according to stitch pattern guides; fill in uncoded areas of C, G and H pieces using forest and Continental Stitch.

2: With forest, Overcast edges of C and cutout edges of G; with mermaid green, Overcast one long edge of J.

3: For Wall Basket, with mermaid green, Whipstitch A and B pieces together as indicated on A graph and according to Wall Basket Assembly Illustration; Overcast unfinished edges. Whipstitch D to back A as indicated.

4: For Tissue Cover, with mermaid green, Whipstitch E and F pieces together; with forest, Whipstitch assembly and G together. With mermaid green, Overcast unfinished edges.

5: For Planter, with forest, Whipstitch short ends of H together as indicated; Whipstitch I to bottom edge of H. Sliding J piece over top edge of H with Overcast edge down, with mermaid green, Whipstitch unfinished top edges of H and J pieces together.

NOTE: Cut one 20" [50.8cm] length each of gold trim, mauve lace and forest lace.

6: Glue gold trim to edges of C as shown in photo, cutting or overlapping trim as needed. Gathering slightly to fit, glue mauve lace to wrong side of C piece 1" [2.5cm] from outer edge; glue forest lace around outer edge of C as shown in photo.

NOTE: Cut one 34" [86.4cm] length each of gold trim, mauve lace and forest lace.

7: Holding edges of mauve and forest lace together, glue laces around Tissue Cover, cutting or overlapping lace as needed; glue trim over top edges of lace, cutting or overlapping trim as needed.

8: With gold thread, sew beads to C, G and H pieces as indicated. Glue flowers to C, G and H pieces as shown; center and glue C over front A.

NOTE: Cut one 14" [35.6cm], one 17" [43.2cm] and one 25" [63.5cm] length each of gold trim, mauve lace and forest lace.

9: Holding edges of 14" trim and laces together, with gold thread, sew to wash-cloth; center and sew three rosebuds over trim as shown. Repeat using 17" lengths for hand towel and 25" lengths for bath towel.✢

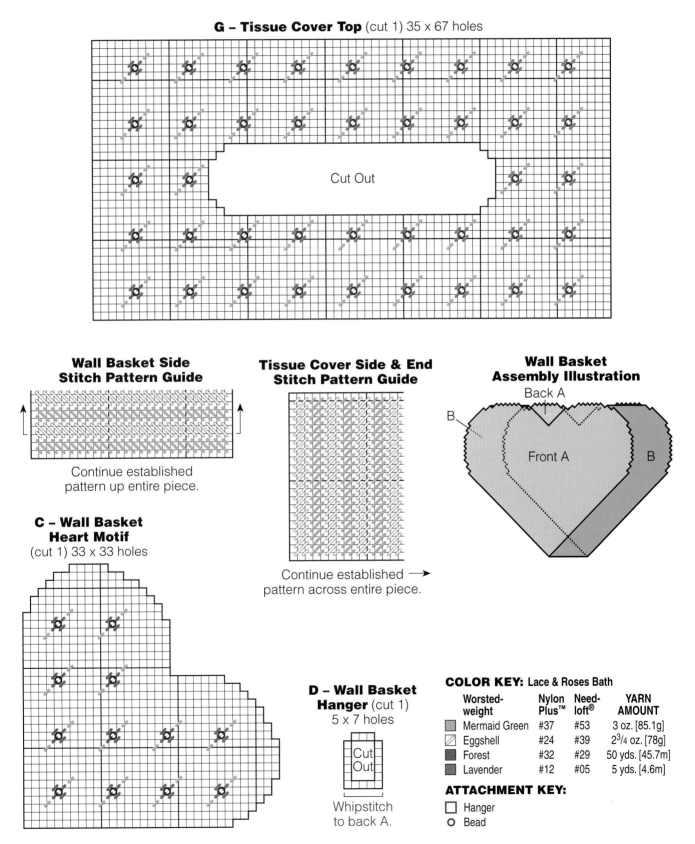

G – Tissue Cover Top (cut 1) 35 x 67 holes

Cut Out

Wall Basket Side Stitch Pattern Guide

Continue established pattern up entire piece.

Tissue Cover Side & End Stitch Pattern Guide

Continue established pattern across entire piece. →

Wall Basket Assembly Illustration

Back A

B

Front A

B

C – Wall Basket Heart Motif
(cut 1) 33 x 33 holes

D – Wall Basket Hanger (cut 1)
5 x 7 holes

Cut Out

Whipstitch to back A.

COLOR KEY: Lace & Roses Bath

Worsted-weight	Nylon Plus™	Need-loft®	YARN AMOUNT
Mermaid Green	#37	#53	3 oz. [85.1g]
Eggshell	#24	#39	2³/₄ oz. [78g]
Forest	#32	#29	50 yds. [45.7m]
Lavender	#12	#05	5 yds. [4.6m]

ATTACHMENT KEY:
☐ Hanger
○ Bead

LACE & ROSES BATH

(Photo on pages 56 & 57.)

(Photo on pages 56 & 57.)

Tip

Touch the heart of any romantic with this gorgeous bath set. Take the lace trim and put it on hand towels to match your pretty powder room. You can even use the heart basket to store photos of your loved ones. Or, fill the planter with individually-wrapped candies and when they're all gone, put pretty flowers in the planter.

COLOR KEY: Lace & Roses Bath

Worsted-weight	Nylon Plus™	Need-loft®	YARN AMOUNT
Mermaid Green	#37	#53	3 oz. [85.1g]
Eggshell	#24	#39	2³/₄ oz. [78g]
Forest	#32	#29	50 yds. [45.7m]
Lavender	#12	#05	5 yds. [4.6m]

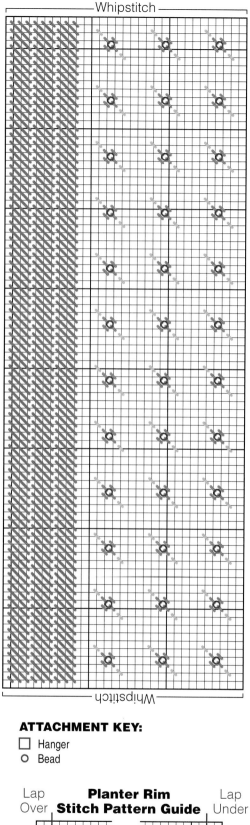

H – Planter Side (cut 1) 31 x 84 holes

Whipstitch

Whipstitch

A – Wall Basket Front & Back
(cut 1 each) 48 x 48 holes

Overcast between arrows.

Whipstitch to one B between arrows.

Whipstitch to one B between arrows.

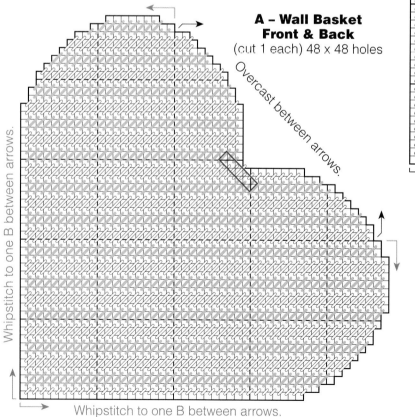

ATTACHMENT KEY:

☐ Hanger
○ Bead

Lap Over

Planter Rim Stitch Pattern Guide

Lap Under

Continue established pattern across unseen area.

TO MY LOVE

*Designed by
Michele Wilcox*

Instructions on next page

TO MY LOVE

(Photo on page 61.)

SIZES: Coaster Holder is 5" square x 1⅝" tall [12.7cm x 4.1cm]; each Coaster is 4⅝" square [11.7cm]; Basket is 4½" square x 3" tall [11.4cm x 7.6cm], not including handle.

MATERIALS: Three sheets of 7-count plastic canvas; Craft glue or glue gun; #3 pearl cotton or six-strand embroidery floss (for amounts see Color Key; Worsted-weight or plastic canvas yarn (for amounts see Color Key).

CUTTING INSTRUCTIONS:

A: For Coasters, cut four 30 x 30 holes.
B: For Coaster Holder bottom, cut one 32 x 32 holes.
C: For Coaster Holder sides, cut two according to graph.
D: For Coaster Holder end pieces, cut four according to graph.
E: For Basket sides, cut four 19 x 29 holes.
F: For Basket bottom, cut one 29 x 29 holes (no graph).
G: For Basket handle, cut one 5 x 89 holes (no graph).

STITCHING INSTRUCTIONS:

1: Using colors and stitches indicated, work A-E pieces according to graphs and F and G pieces according to stitch pattern guides; with black yarn, Overcast edges of A and G pieces.
2: Using pearl cotton or six strands floss in colors and embroidery stitches indicated, embroider detail on E pieces as indicated on graphs.
3: With black yarn, Whipstitch B-D pieces together as indicated and according to Coaster Holder Assembly Illustration; Overcast unfinished edges.
4: Whipstitch E and F pieces together as indicated and according to Basket Assembly Illustration; Overcast unfinished edges. Glue ends of G to opposite sides of Basket.✢

A – Coaster (cut 4) 30 x 30 holes

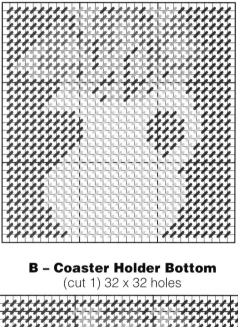

B – Coaster Holder Bottom
(cut 1) 32 x 32 holes

Tip

Yummy! Who could resist this sweet container? Fill this sweet treat basket with chocolate, caramel, peppermints, after-dinner mints or even jewelry! It's great for almost anything you want to put in it.

COLOR KEY: To My Love

#3 pearl cotton or floss	AMOUNT
■ Black	6 yds. [5.5m]
☐ Yellow	4 yds. [3.7m]

Worsted-weight	Nylon Plus™	Need-loft®	YARN AMOUNT
■ Black	#02	#00	2¾ oz. [78g]
☐ Straw	#41	#19	25 yds. [22.9m]
▨ Mermaid Green	#37	#53	17 yds. [15.5m]
▨ Watermelon	#54	#55	15 yds. [13.7m]
◨ Eggshell	#24	#39	9 yds. [8.2m]
☐ Pink	#11	#07	5 yds. [4.6m]
■ Crimsom	#53	#42	4 yds. [3.7m]
▨ Tangerine	#15	#11	3 yds. [2.7m]

STITCH KEY:
— Backstitch/Straight
● French Knot

Basket Bottom Stitch Pattern Guide

Continue established pattern up and across entire piece.

Basket Handle Stitch Pattern Guide

Continue established pattern across entire piece.

E – Basket Side (cut 4) 19 x 29 holes

D – Coaster Holder End Piece
(cut 4) 6 x 14 holes

Whipstitch to C.
Whipstitch to B.

Coaster Holder Assembly Illustration

C – Coaster Holder Side
(cut 2) 10 x 32 holes

Cut Out

Whipstitch to one D.
Whipstitch to one D.
Whipstitch to B.

Basket Assembly Illustration

G

E
E
E
E
F

Gift Idea

Here's a great gift for anyone on your list! There's something about flowers that just brightens everyone's day, so why not fill a wicker basket with colorful, silk flowers. Then, among the stems, place coasters, a large mug and hot drink packets. If you're giving cocoa, you might want to also give a small bag of marshmallows to go with it. Or if you're presenting tea, try some honey sticks or cinnamon sticks to stir in.

SWEETHEART SCENTS

Designed by Patricia Hall

SIZE: About 18" long [45.7cm].

MATERIALS: One sheet of 7-count plastic canvas; ¼ sheet of 10-count plastic canvas; ½ yd. [0.5m] of white 6"-wide [15.2cm] fine-gauge nylon tulle; 1⅓ yds. [3m] of pink ¼" [6mm] satin ribbon; 1⅔ yds. [1.5m] of pink 1½" [3.8cm] satin ribbon; 2 yds. [1.8m] of light pink 3mm pearl strand; One 2" [5.1cm] metal ring; Four pink ¾" [19mm] iridescent ribbon roses; One package rose-scented paper sachet; Craft glue or glue gun; #3 pearl cotton or six-strand embroidery floss (for amount see Color Key); Worsted-weight or plastic canvas yarn (for amounts see Color Key).

CUTTING INSTRUCTIONS:

NOTES: Use 7-count for A-D and 10-count canvas for E pieces.

Graphs continued on page 66.

A: For Small Sachet fronts, cut three according to graph.

B: For Small Sachet backs, cut three according to graph.

C: For Large Sachet front, cut one according to graph.

D: For Large Sachet back, cut one according to graph.

E: For leaves, cut eight according to graph.

STITCHING INSTRUCTIONS:

1: Using yarn and pearl cotton or six strands floss in colors and stitches indicated, work A, C and E pieces according to graphs; using white and Continental Stitch, work B and D pieces.

2: With matching colors as shown in photo, Overcast cutout edges of A and C pieces and edges of E pieces.

3: Using crimson (Separate into individual plies, if desired.) and Backstitch, embroider detail (Center letters and numbers of choice within boxed areas.) on one B and D pieces as indicated on graphs and Letter and Number Graphs.

NOTE: Cut one 12" [30.5cm] and one 26" [66cm] length of narrow ribbon.

4: Assemble B and D pieces, narrow ribbon, wide ribbon and metal ring according to Wall Hanging Assembly Diagram on page 67.

NOTES: Cut four 18" [45.7cm] lengths of pearl strand.

Using A and C pieces as patterns, cut three small hearts and one large heart from tulle.

5: For each Small Sachet (make three), with white, Whipstitch and assemble one small tulle heart, one pearl strand, one ribbon rose, a small amount of paper sachet, one A, one B and two E pieces according to Sachet Assembly Diagram on page 67.

6: For Large Sachet (make one), Whipstitch and assemble large tulle heart, remaining pearl strand, ribbon rose, paper sachet, C, D and two remaining E pieces according to diagram.✚

Number Graph

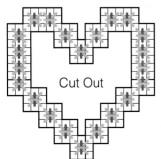

STITCH KEY:
— Backstitch/Straight
☐ Letter/Number Placement

E – Leaf
(cut 8 from 10-count)
5 x 7 holes

A – Small Sachet Front
(cut 3 from 7-count)
19 x 19 holes

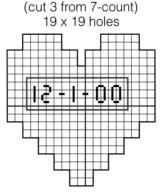

Cut Out

B – Small Sachet Back
(cut 3 from 7-count)
19 x 19 holes

12 - 1 - 00

COLOR KEY: Sweetheart Scents

#3 pearl cotton or floss			AMOUNT
☐ Green			4 yds. [3.7m]

Worsted-weight	Nylon Plus™	Need-loft®	YARN AMOUNT
☐ White	#01	#41	55 yds. [50.3m]
■ Lavender	#12	#05	16 yds. [14.6m]
▨ Pink	#11	#07	16 yds. [14.6m]
■ Crimson	#53	#42	3 yds. [2.7m]

SWEETHEART SCENTS

(Instructions & photo on pages 64 & 65.)

(Instructions & photo on pages 64 & 65.)

Letter Graph

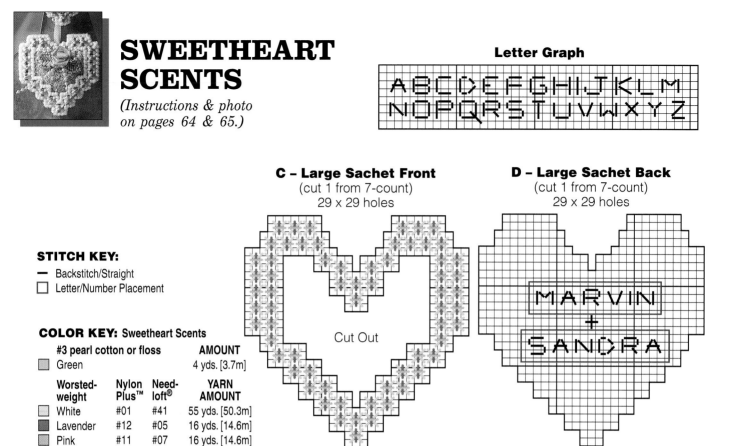

STITCH KEY:
- Backstitch/Straight
- ☐ Letter/Number Placement

COLOR KEY: Sweetheart Scents

#3 pearl cotton or floss			AMOUNT
☐ Green			4 yds. [3.7m]

Worsted-weight	Nylon Plus™	Need-loft®	YARN AMOUNT
☐ White	#01	#41	55 yds. [50.3m]
☐ Lavender	#12	#05	16 yds. [14.6m]
☐ Pink	#11	#07	16 yds. [14.6m]
■ Crimson	#53	#42	3 yds. [2.7m]

C – Large Sachet Front
(cut 1 from 7-count)
29 x 29 holes

Cut Out

D – Large Sachet Back
(cut 1 from 7-count)
29 x 29 holes

MARVIN + SANDRA

Heartwarming Story

One of my friends' parents ran away to Mexico to elope when they were just seventeen years old. Because they didn't have a formal wedding, they bought each other a silk bag to put a garter and tie, rings and flowers in, as a token of their mutual affection. On their way back home, they had a lay-over in the airport because of stormy weather, and accidentally fell asleep in the terminal chairs. While they dozed, a thief stole some of their luggage, which contained their nuptial bags. When they arrived home, the bride's sister made them new silk bags, except this time without the wedding items. Since the rings and other items were lost for good, she filled the bags with potpourri. These bags now hold a place of honor, enclosed in a glass case on a bookshelf in their living room, where all can see and appreciate the handiwork of a sister's love, and the love story behind them. Although the tokens of their affection were stolen so many years ago, their love endures as they celebrate their 27th wedding anniversary this year. – Kim Votaw

Wall Hanging Assembly Diagram
Step 1:
Glue ends of long narrow ribbon to wrong sides of D and one B; glue ends of short narrow ribbon to wrong side of remaining B pieces.

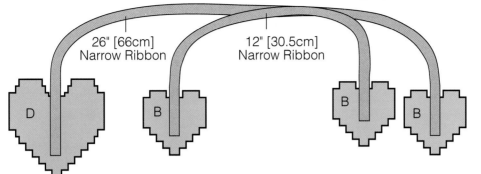

26" [66cm] Narrow Ribbon

12" [30.5cm] Narrow Ribbon

Step 2:
Tie narrow ribbons to metal ring with a Lark's Head Knot; adjust ribbons so that sachets hang at lengths indicated. (**NOTE:** Measurements reflect distance between metal ring and top edge of each sachet.)

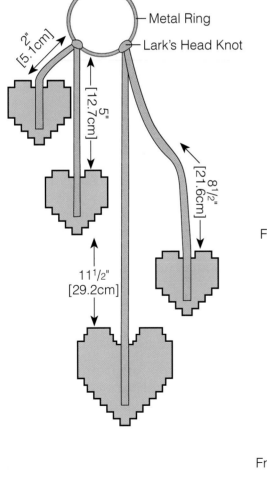

Metal Ring

Lark's Head Knot

2" [5.1cm]

5" [12.7cm]

8½" [21.6cm]

11½" [29.2cm]

Step 3:
Tie wide ribbon into a four-looped bow over narrow ribbons, leaving 5" [12.7cm] tails.

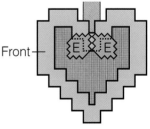

(Sachets not shown.)

Wide Ribbon

5" Tail

5" Tail

Narrow Ribbons

Sachet Assembly Diagram
Step 1:
Glue tulle heart to wrong side of front.

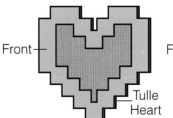

Front

Tulle Heart

Step 3:
Glue E pieces to front.

Front

Step 2:
Whipstitch front and back pieces wrong sides together, filling with paper sachet before closing.

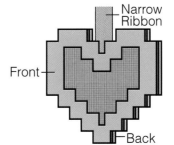

Narrow Ribbon

Front

Back

Step 4:
Tie pearl strand into a bow; glue pearl bow and rose to front.

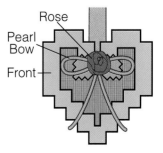

Rose

Pearl Bow

Front

RIBBON ROSE BOX

Designed by Debbie Tabor

SIZE: 4³⁄₈" x 4½" x 1¾" tall [11.1cm x 11.4cm x 4.4cm].

MATERIALS: Two sheets of 10-count plastic canvas; Silk ribbon (for amount see Color Key); Six-strand embroidery floss (for amounts see Color Key); Worsted-weight or plastic canvas yarn (for amount see Color Key).

CUTTING INSTRUCTIONS:

A: For side, cut one 15 x 135 holes (no graph).
B: For top pieces #1-#4, cut one each according to graphs.
C: For divider piece #1, cut one according to graph.
D: For divider piece #2, cut one according to graph.
E: For bottom, cut one according to graph.

STITCHING INSTRUCTIONS:

NOTES: C-E pieces are not worked. Separate yarn into individual plies.
1: Using six strands floss in colors indicated and Continental Stitch, work B pieces according to graphs; fill in uncoded areas of B pieces and work A using eggshell and Continental Stitch. Overcast indicated edges of B pieces.
2: Using ribbon and floss (six strands for leaves and borders on A and two strands for stems on B pieces) in colors and embroidery stitches indicated, embroider detail on A and B pieces as indicated on graphs.
3: With eggshell, Whipstitch A-E pieces together as indicated on graphs and according to Trinket Box Assembly Diagram on page 70.✝

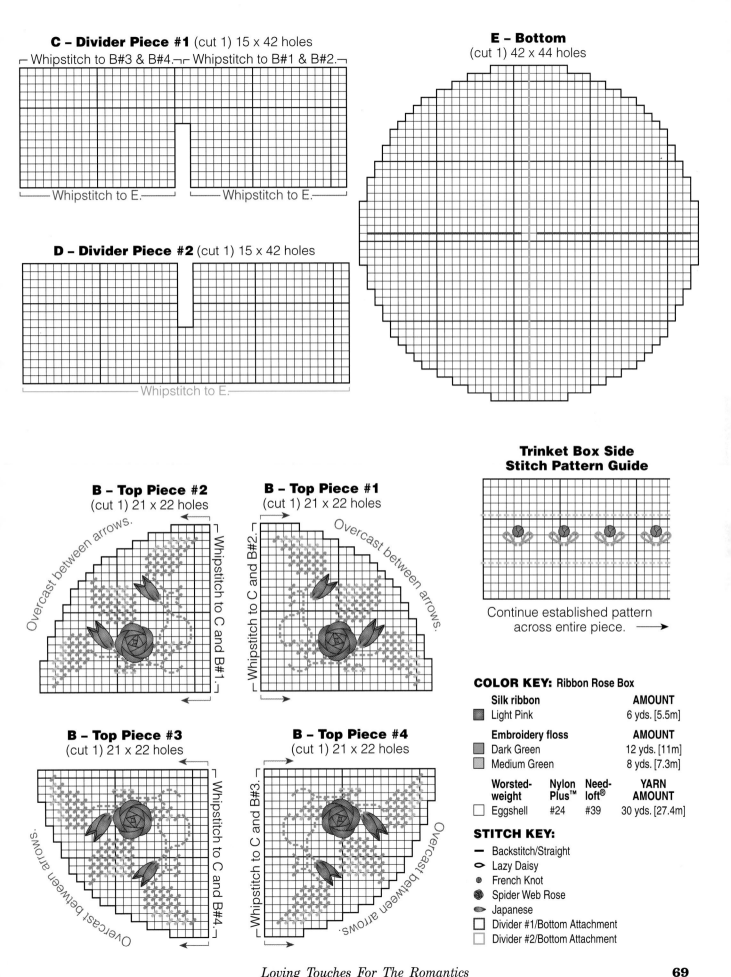

C – Divider Piece #1 (cut 1) 15 x 42 holes

⌐ Whipstitch to B#3 & B#4.⌐⌐ Whipstitch to B#1 & B#2.⌐

└ Whipstitch to E.┘   └ Whipstitch to E.┘

D – Divider Piece #2 (cut 1) 15 x 42 holes

└ Whipstitch to E.┘

E – Bottom
(cut 1) 42 x 44 holes

B – Top Piece #2
(cut 1) 21 x 22 holes

Overcast between arrows.

Whipstitch to C and B#1.

B – Top Piece #1
(cut 1) 21 x 22 holes

Overcast between arrows.

Whipstitch to C and B#2.

B – Top Piece #3
(cut 1) 21 x 22 holes

Overcast between arrows.

Whipstitch to C and B#4.

B – Top Piece #4
(cut 1) 21 x 22 holes

Whipstitch to C and B#3.

Overcast between arrows.

Trinket Box Side Stitch Pattern Guide

Continue established pattern across entire piece. →

COLOR KEY: Ribbon Rose Box

Silk ribbon			AMOUNT
■ Light Pink			6 yds. [5.5m]

Embroidery floss			AMOUNT
■ Dark Green			12 yds. [11m]
■ Medium Green			8 yds. [7.3m]

Worsted-weight	Nylon Plus™	Need-loft®	YARN AMOUNT
□ Eggshell	#24	#39	30 yds. [27.4m]

STITCH KEY:
- ▬ Backstitch/Straight
- ∽ Lazy Daisy
- • French Knot
- ✹ Spider Web Rose
- ⬬ Japanese
- ☐ Divider #1/Bottom Attachment
- ☐ Divider #2/Bottom Attachment

Loving Touches For The Romantics

RIBBON ROSE BOX

(Photo on page 68.)

Spider Web Rose

French Knot

Japanese Stitch

Trinket Box Assembly Diagram
(Pieces are shown in different colors for contrast.)

Step 1:
Interlock C and D
pieces, forming divider.

Step 2:
Whipstitch bottom
edges of divider to E.

Step 3:
Whipstitch short ends of A together,
forming side; matching up seam
edges of side with one divider,
Whipstitch bottom edges of A to E.

Step 4:
Whipstitch indicated edges of
B pieces together and to C;
Overcast unfinished edges.

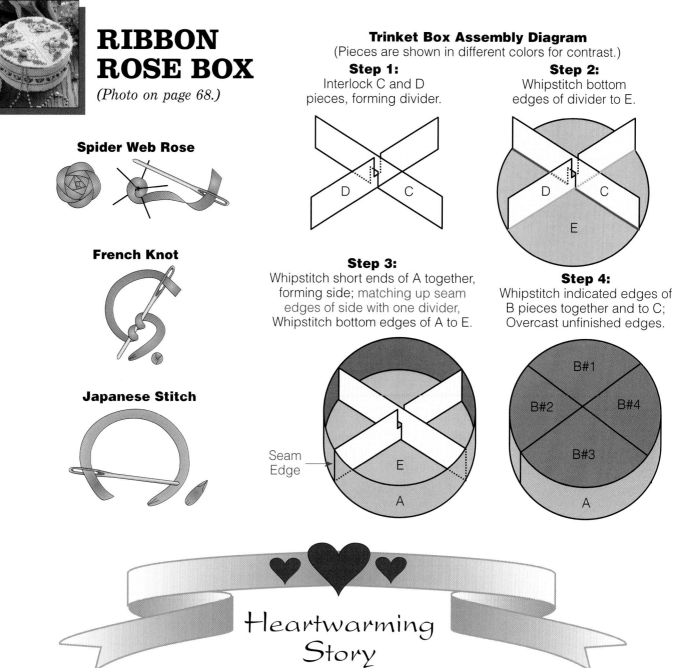

Heartwarming Story

When my great-grandmother was very ill, she sent my grandmother and mother up to her attic to retrieve a large cedar chest. She said that she wanted to give each of us children a special gift to remember her by. As my mother and grandmother pulled items out of the chest, my great-grandmother briefly told us stories about each. When she gave her father's Civil War hat to my brother, she told of his bittersweet homecoming. Then, she presented my sister with an antique glass oil lamp that brought tears to her eyes as she related the memories it held. When my turn came, she paused before she handed me a small, golden box with an ivory-plated lid. On the top, a splash of flowers lined the rim, with a yellow rose in the center. My great-grandmother tearfully told us that it was the first gift my great-grandfather had given her. When she gave me that little box, she was handing to me all of the emotions and memories that it held, as well as the little silver ring I was surprised to find in it when I brought it home. – Kim Votaw

HEARTS & CROSSES

(Photo on page 71.)

SIZES: Wall Pocket is 1½" x 7½" x 6½" tall [3.8cm x 19cm x 16.5cm]; Cross is 7½" x 10¾" [19cm x 27.3cm], not including photo album.

MATERIALS: Two sheets of 7-count plastic canvas; ½ sheet of white 7-count plastic canvas; 10" x 11½" [25.4cm x 29.2cm] three-ring photo album; ½ yd. [0.5m] of off-white satin fabric with gold cupid print (or fabric of choice); Batting; 1⅓ yds. [1.2m] each of candlelight 1⅛" [2.9cm] lace and white/gold/burgundy ½" [13mm] trim; 1 yd. [0.9m] of white ⅝" [16mm] satin ribbon; 6" [15.2cm] of gold metallic cord; Craft glue or glue gun; Worsted-weight or plastic canvas yarn (for amounts see Color Key).

CUTTING INSTRUCTIONS:

A: For Wall Pocket front, cut one from clear according to graph.
B: For Wall Pocket back, cut one from white according to graph.
C: For Wall Pocket sides, cut two from clear according to graph.
D: For Wall Pocket bow loops, cut two from clear according to graph.
E: For Wall Pocket bow tails, cut two from clear according to graph.
F: For Cross, cut one from clear according to graph.

STITCHING INSTRUCTIONS:

NOTE: B piece is not worked.
1: Using colors and stitches indicated, work A, C-E (one E on opposite side of canvas) and F pieces according to graphs; with matching colors, Overcast edges of E and F pieces.
2: For Wall Pocket, with crimson, Whipstitch A-C pieces together as indicated on graphs and according to Wall Pocket Assembly Illustration; Overcast unfinished edges of A and C pieces.
NOTE: Cut one 1⅓-yd. [1.2m] length of crimson.

3: For bow, Whipstitch and assemble D pieces and strand according to Bow Assembly Diagram; glue bow and bow tails to Pocket front as shown in photo.
NOTE: Cut cord in half.
4: Overlap ends of one cord strand ½" [13mm] and glue to secure, forming one ring; repeat with remaining cord.
NOTE: Cut one 3" [7.6cm] and one 12" [30.5cm] length of ribbon.
5: Tie 12" ribbon into a bow; trim ends as desired. Assemble bow, 3" ribbon and rings according to Ribbon & Ring Motif Assembly Diagram; glue motif to Cross as shown.
6: Using album cover as a pattern, cut several thicknesses of batting; glue batting to cover. Cover album with fabric. Glue lace and trim to album front as shown.
7: Center and glue Cross to album front.
NOTE: Cut remaining ribbon in half.
8: Glue each ribbon 2" [5.1cm] inside front and back covers. Tie ribbons into a bow to close album; trim ends of bow as desired.✣

COLOR KEY: Hearts & Crosses

	Worsted-weight	Nylon Plus™	Needloft®	YARN AMOUNT
■	Lavender	#12	#05	25 yds. [22.9m]
■	Crimson	#53	#42	10 yds. [9.1m]
■	Pink	#11	#07	10 yds. [9.1m]
■	Burgundy	#13	#03	8 yds. [7.3m]

A – Wall Pocket Front
(cut 1 from clear) 33 x 33 holes

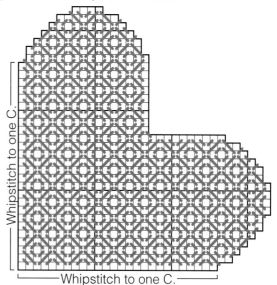

Whipstitch to one C.

Whipstitch to one C.

Loving Touches For The Romantics

Ribbon & Ring Motif Assembly Diagram

Step 1:
Fold 3" [7.6cm] ribbon over twice lengthwise, forming a flat shaft; glue to secure.

3"

(first fold)   (second fold)

Shaft

Step 2:
Thread rings onto ribbon shaft.

Shaft

Rings

Step 3:
Fold shaft in half; glue short ends together.

Step 4:
Glue bow over ends of shaft.

Wall Pocket Assembly Illustration

B

A

C   C

Bow Assembly Diagram

Step 1:
With crimson, Whipstitch short ends of D pieces together; Overcast unfinished edges.

D   D

Step 2:
Wrap entire strand around center of bow; secure ends under wraps.

Yarn

STITCH KEY:
☐ Side/Back Attachment

F – Cross
(cut 1 from clear)
49 x 71 holes

E – Wall Pocket Bow Tail
(cut 2 from clear)
5 x 21 holes

B – Wall Pocket Back
(cut 1 from white) 42 x 42 holes

Cut out gray areas carefully.

C – Side
(cut 2 from clear)
8 x 26 holes
Whipstitch to B.
Whipstitch to A.

D – Wall Pocket Bow Loop
(cut 2 from clear) 3 x 29 holes

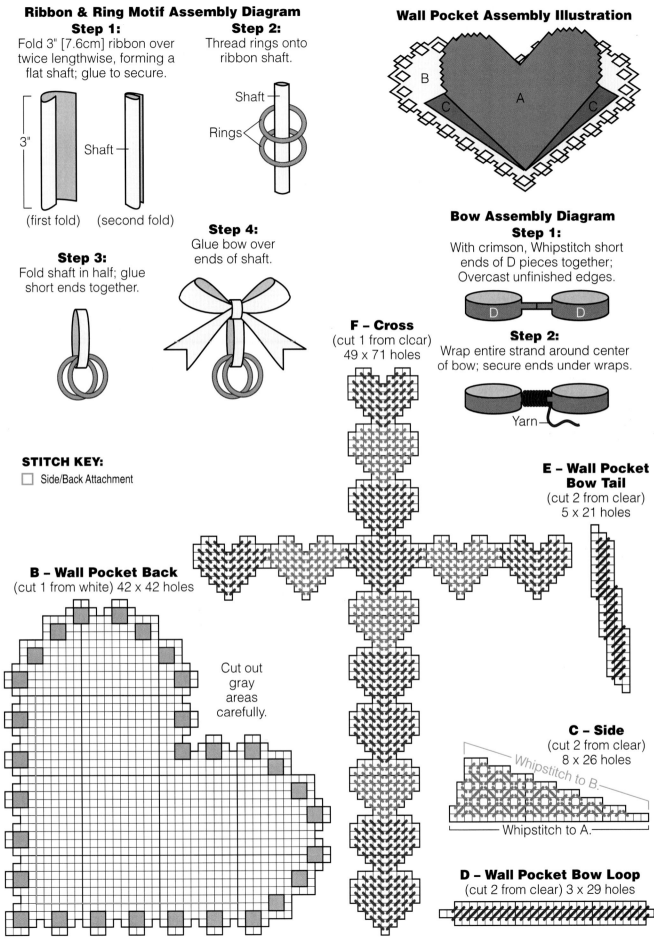

Loving Touches For The Romantics

Tasty Creations for the Cook

Chapter Four

SIZE: 3⅞" x 6¼" x 4½" tall [9.8cm x 15.9cm x 11.4cm], not including handle.

MATERIALS: Two sheets of 7-count plastic canvas; Craft glue or glue gun; Worsted-weight or plastic canvas yarn (for amounts see Color Key).

CUTTING INSTRUCTIONS:
A: For Basket sides, cut two 29 x 41 holes (no graph).
B: For Basket ends, cut two 25 x 29 holes (no graph).

C: For Basket bottom, cut one 25 x 41 holes (no graph).
D: For Basket handle, cut one 5 x 89 holes (no graph).
E: For leaf, cut one according to graph.
F: For stem, cut one according to graph.
G: For grapes, cut twelve according to graph.
H: For orange, cut one according to graph.
I: For apple, cut one according to graph.
J: For banana, cut one according to graph.

STITCHING INSTRUCTIONS:

1: Using colors and stitches indicated, work pieces according to graphs and stitch pattern guides; with matching colors as shown in photo, Overcast unfinished edges of D and E-J pieces.

2: With gold, Whipstitch A-C pieces together, forming Basket; Overcast unfinished edges.

3: Glue one end of D to inside of each Basket side; glue E-J pieces to one Basket side as shown or as desired.✣

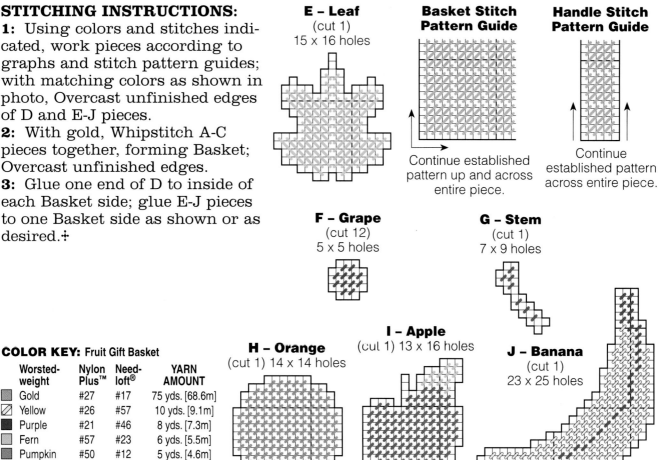

E – Leaf
(cut 1)
15 x 16 holes

Basket Stitch Pattern Guide

Continue established pattern up and across entire piece.

Handle Stitch Pattern Guide

Continue established pattern across entire piece.

F – Grape
(cut 12)
5 x 5 holes

G – Stem
(cut 1)
7 x 9 holes

H – Orange
(cut 1) 14 x 14 holes

I – Apple
(cut 1) 13 x 16 holes

J – Banana
(cut 1)
23 x 25 holes

COLOR KEY: Fruit Gift Basket

	Worsted-weight	Nylon Plus™	Need-loft®	YARN AMOUNT
	Gold	#27	#17	75 yds. [68.6m]
	Yellow	#26	#57	10 yds. [9.1m]
	Purple	#21	#46	8 yds. [7.3m]
	Fern	#57	#23	6 yds. [5.5m]
	Pumpkin	#50	#12	5 yds. [4.6m]
	Red	#20	#01	5 yds. [4.6m]
	Cinnamon	#44	#14	4 yds. [3.7m]

Christmas Cooking!

The sweet and savory flavors of fruit can tempt any appetite. Whatever you choose to fill this lovely basket with, make sure to put in some of these healthy, home-made fruit rolls as a little something extra.

Recipe from the kitchen of Christmas Companion

Fruit Rolls

Skin and pit 5 or 6 whole apricots, pears or peaches. Blend them until the mixture is a smooth puree. Add a splash of lemon to prevent rapid browning. Depending on how much fruit is blended, gather an appropriate number of baking or dehydrating trays (flat, plastic trays with upturned edges work best) to cover the bottom of the tray with about ⅛" thickness of the blended fruit. Very lightly oil the trays, then pour the puree on each tray. Put trays in a dehydrator if you have one, or set them outside in the sunshine (covered with a screen or netting to keep out other natural ingredients, such as flies). When the mixture is dried to your satisfaction, slice the dried fruit into long strips, cutting lengthwise on the tray. Then, pull the strips up off the tray while rolling them into long fruit rolls.

GLITTERY ACCENTS

Designed by Eileen Pearl

SIZES: Each Coaster is 4½" [11.4cm] square; Trivet is 10¾" [27.3cm] square.

MATERIALS: Two sheets of 7-count plastic canvas; Glitter yarn (for amounts see Color Key), or use worsted-weight or plastic canvas yarn.

CUTTING INSTRUCTIONS:
A: For Coasters, cut four according to graph.

B: For Trivet, cut one according to graph.

STITCHING INSTRUCTIONS:
Using colors and stitches indicated, work pieces according to graphs; with matching colors, Overcast unfinished edges.✝

Decorate your table with glitter this Christmas.
There's nothing like a beautiful table setting and good food
to put you in the Holiday mood. Make something delicious
to be set on these sparkling coasters.

COLOR KEY: Glittery Accents

Worsted-weight	Nylon Plus™	Need-loft®	YARN AMOUNT
▨ Green Glitter	#31	#27	50 yds. [45.7m]
▨ White Glitter	#01	#41	50 yds. [45.7m]

A – Coaster
(cut 4) 29 x 29 holes

Recipe from the kitchen of Christmas Companion

Hot Cranberry Fruit Punch

- •4 cups cranberry juice
- •2 cups orange juice
- •2 tbsps. lemon juice
- •2 tbsps. sugar
- •2 tsp. cinnamon
- •2 shakes of ground cloves

Mix all ingredients; bring to a boil, lower temperature and simmer for twenty minutes.

B – Trivet
(cut 1) 70 x 71 holes

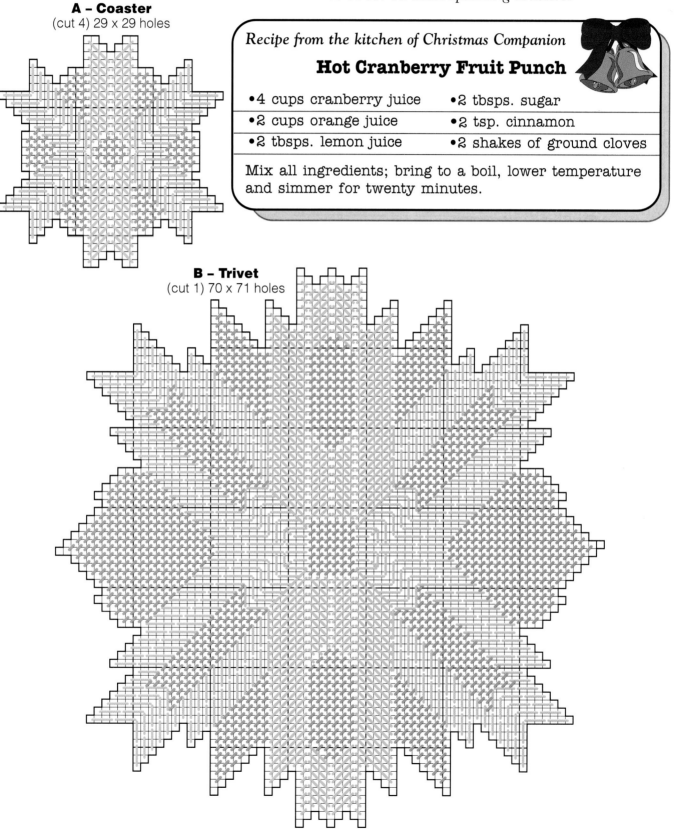

Gift Idea

Try this suncatcher as a unique package topper for someone who loves to cook. Use this bee to top a gift basket filled with cookie cutters, a cute timer, a spoon holder, a bag of flavored honey sticks or a new pair of oven mitts.

SIZE: 6⅜" x 7½" [16.2cm x 19cm], not including hanger.

MATERIALS: One sheet of 7-count plastic canvas; 1 yd. of [0.9m] white ⅛" [3mm] satin ribbon; Pearlized cord (for amount see Color Key); Worsted-weight or plastic canvas yarn (for amounts see Color Key).

CUTTING INSTRUCTIONS:
For Suncatcher sides, cut two according to graph.

STITCHING INSTRUCTIONS:
1: Using colors indicated and Continental Stitch, work pieces according to graph.

2: With matching colors, Whipstitch pieces wrong sides together.
3: Using Lark's Head Knot, tie ribbon through upper cutout. Tie ribbon ends into a bow; trim ends as desired.✝

Suncatcher Side
(cut 2) 42 x 50 holes
Cut out gray areas carefully.

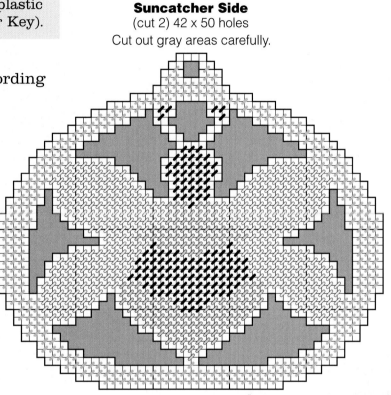

COLOR KEY: Bee Suncatcher

Pearlized cord			AMOUNT
▨ White			25 yds. [22.9m]

Worsted-weight	Nylon Plus™	Need-loft®	YARN AMOUNT
▨ Cerulean	#04	#35	40 yds. [36.6m]
■ Black	#02	#00	12 yds. [11m]
▨ Yellow	#26	#57	12 yds. [11m]

Christmas Cooking

With so many busy people, wouldn't it be nice to treat someone who always works overtime? That cook in your life would love to have special gifts, too. Best of all, here's an easy, but very delicious, recipe for all those workers and drones out there with a busy schedule.

Recipe from the kitchen of Christmas Companion
Honey Bee Ambrosia

•4 oranges	•¼ cup honey
•1 banana	•2 tbsps. lemon juice
•½ cup orange juice	•¼ cup flaked coconut

Pare oranges. Cut crosswise into thin slices and place in a serving bowl. Peel banana and cut into thin slices and place in bowl with oranges. Toss fruits. Blend orange juice, honey and lemon juice and pour over fruits. Sprinkle with coconut.

GOODIE BASKETS

Designed by Betty Frew

SIZE: Holds a 3½" x 6" x 2" tall [8.9cm x 15.2cm x 5.1cm] mini-loaf pan.

MATERIALS FOR ONE: One sheet of white 7-count white plastic canvas; Metallic cord (for amount see Color Key); Worsted-weight or plastic canvas yarn (for amounts see Color Key).

CUTTING INSTRUCTIONS:
A: For side, cut one according to graph.

B: For ends, cut two 12 x 22 holes.
C: For bottom, cut one 22 x 38 holes (no graph).

STITCHING INSTRUCTIONS:
NOTE: C piece is not worked.
1: Using colors and stitches indicated, work A and B pieces according to graphs; if desired, fill in uncoded areas using white and Continental Stitch.
2: With white, Whipstitch A-C pieces together as indicated on graphs; if desired, Overcast unfinished edges.‡

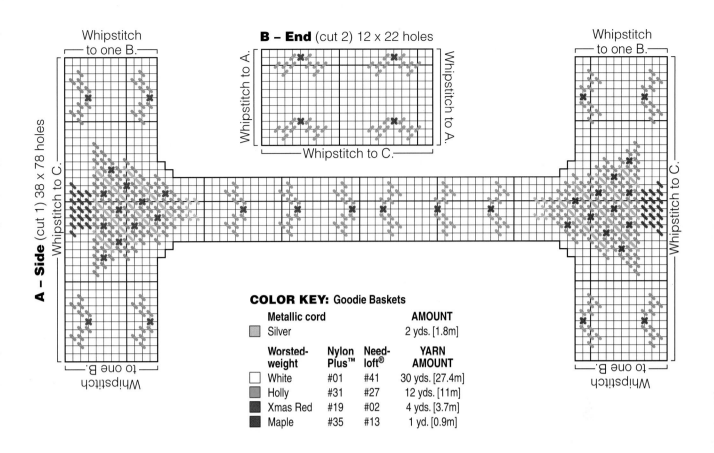

A – Side (cut 1) 38 x 78 holes

Whipstitch to one B.

Whipstitch to C.

Whipstitch to one B.

B – End (cut 2) 12 x 22 holes

Whipstitch to A.

Whipstitch to A.

Whipstitch to C.

Whipstitch to one B.

Whipstitch to C.

Whipstitch to one B.

COLOR KEY: Goodie Baskets

Metallic cord			AMOUNT
▨ Silver			2 yds. [1.8m]

Worsted-weight	Nylon Plus™	Need-loft®	YARN AMOUNT
☐ White	#01	#41	30 yds. [27.4m]
▨ Holly	#31	#27	12 yds. [11m]
■ Xmas Red	#19	#02	4 yds. [3.7m]
■ Maple	#35	#13	1 yd. [0.9m]

Christmas Cooking

Surprise someone you love with a gift from the heart. These Christmas Goodie Baskets are just begging to be filled with some delectable baked goodies. Now you'll just have to try this delicious Apricot Nut Bread for yourself!

Recipe from the kitchen of Christmas Companion

Apricot Nut Bread

- 4 tbsps. butter
- 1 cup sugar
- 1 egg
- ¾ cup milk
- 3 cups flour
- 3½ tsps. baking powder
- ¾ tsp. salt
- 1 cup sliced apricot halves
- 1 cup chopped or whole pecans

Cover sliced apricots with boiling water. Let stand while mixing other ingredients. Mix softened butter and sugar together, beat one egg into sugar and butter mixture until sugar is dissolved. Add milk and mix. Mix dry ingredients together. Slowly beat dry ingredients into batter. Drain apricots; fold nuts and apricots into batter. Spoon into three mini loaf pans. Bake 45 minutes at 350 degrees, or until knife inserted in center comes out clean.

Designed by
Kristine Loffredo

SIZES: Centerpiece is 10⅜" square x 11" tall [26.3cm x 27.9cm]; Holder is 6½" x 7⅜" x 8" tall [16.5cm x 18.7cm x 20.3cm]; each Napkin Ring Tree Motif is 2" x 2½" [5.1cm x 6.4cm].

MATERIALS FOR ENTIRE SET: Six sheets of 7-count plastic canvas; Craft glue or glue gun; Worsted-weight or plastic canvas yarn (for amounts see Color Key on page 86).

NOTE: Graphs on pages 86-88.

CENTERPIECE
CUTTING INSTRUCTIONS:

A: For Centerpiece side pieces #1 and #2, cut four each according to graphs.
B: For Centerpiece basket bottom, cut one 43 x 44 holes.
C: For Centerpiece basket side pieces, cut two 5 x 43 holes and two 5 x 44 holes.

STITCHING INSTRUCTIONS:

1: Using colors and stitches indicated, work pieces according to graphs.
2: With matching colors, Whipstitch and assemble pieces according to Centerpiece Assembly Diagram on page 86.

NAPKIN HOLDER & RING
CUTTING INSTRUCTIONS:

A: For Napkin Holder side pieces, cut two according to graphs.
B: For Napkin Holder bottom, cut one according to graph.
C: For Napkin Holder bottom side pieces, cut six 5 x 13 holes.
D: For Napkin Ring Tree Motifs, cut two according to graphs.
E: For Napkin Rings, cut two 3 x 40 holes.

STITCHING INSTRUCTIONS:

1: Using colors and stitches indicated, work pieces (overlap ends of E pieces as indicated on graph and work through both thicknesses at overlap area to join) according to graphs; with matching colors, Overcast edges of D and E pieces.
2: With holly, Whipstitch A-C pieces together as indicated on graphs and according to Napkin Holder Assembly Illustration on page 88; with matching colors as shown in photo, Overcast unfinished edges. Glue top edges of A pieces together.
4: Glue D and E pieces together as shown in photo.✢

Christmas Cooking

Accent this table set with something to really tempt your taste buds. Here's some yummy, minty fudge to munch on this holiday season!

Recipe from the kitchen of Christmas Companion

Minty Fudge

- Three 6-oz. packages of semi-sweet chocolates chips
- 14-oz. can Eagle Brand® sweetened, condensed milk
- ¼ tsp. (or more if desired) peppermint flavoring
- ½ cup chopped nuts (optional)
- Two (or more) crushed peppermint candy canes (optional)

In a heavy saucepan, over low heat, melt chips with condensed milk. Remove from heat. Stir in flavoring and nuts. Spread evenly into waxpaper lined 8-inch square pan. Chill 2 to 3 hours, or until firm. Turn fudge onto cutting board. Peel off wax paper, sprinkle on the crushed peppermint and cut the fudge into squares. Makes 1¾ lbs.

HOLIDAY TABLE

(Instructions & photo on pages 84 & 85.)

COLOR KEY: Holiday Table

Worsted-weight	Nylon Plus™	Need-loft®	YARN AMOUNT
☐ Holly	#31	#27	4 1/2 oz. [127.6g]
☐ White	#01	#41	80 yds. [73.2m]

B – Centerpiece Basket Bottom (cut 1) 43 x 44 holes

Centerpiece Assembly Diagram
(Pieces are shown in different colors for contrast; gray denotes wrong side.)

Step 1:
For each tree section (make four), holding one A#1 and one A#2 wrong sides together and omitting attachment edges, with matching colors, Whipstitch together.

Step 2:
Whipstitch tree sections together through all thicknesses at indicated edges.

Step 3:
With holly, Whipstitch B and C pieces together, forming basket; Overcast unfinished edges.

Step 4:
Place basket inside tree (Turn basket on side to fit through opening in tree, then turn basket upright.); glue to secure.

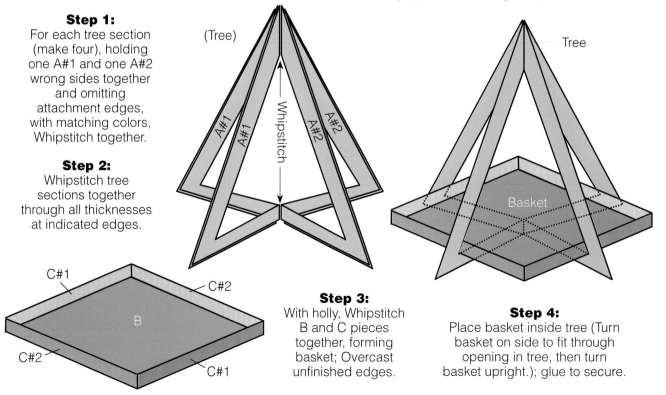

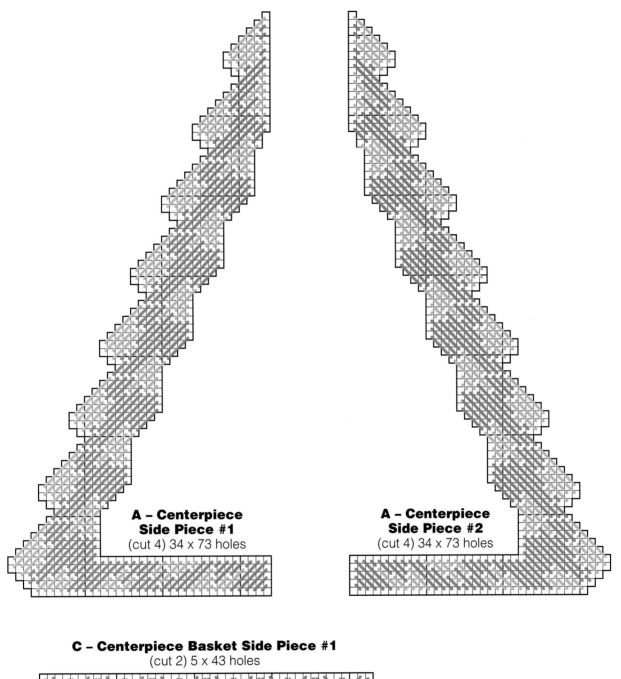

**A – Centerpiece
Side Piece #1**
(cut 4) 34 x 73 holes

**A – Centerpiece
Side Piece #2**
(cut 4) 34 x 73 holes

C – Centerpiece Basket Side Piece #1
(cut 2) 5 x 43 holes

C – Centerpiece Basket Side Piece #2
(cut 2) 5 x 44 holes

**D – Napkin Ring
Tree Motif**
(cut 2) 13 x 16 holes

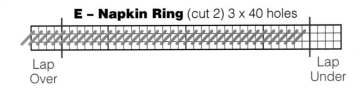

E – Napkin Ring (cut 2) 3 x 40 holes

Lap
Over

Lap
Under

Tasty Creations For The Cook

HOLIDAY TABLE

(Instructions & photo on pages 84 & 85.)

B – Napkin Holder Bottom
(cut 1) 42 x 49 holes

Whipstitch to one C.

Whipstitch to one C.
Whipstitch to one C.
Whipstitch to one A.
Whipstitch to one A.
Whipstitch to one A.
Whipstitch to one A.
Whipstitch to one C.
Whipstitch to one C.
Whipstitch to one C.

COLOR KEY: Holiday Table

	Worsted-weight	Nylon Plus™	Need-loft®	YARN AMOUNT
■ Holly		#31	#27	4¹/₂ oz. [127.6g]
■ White		#01	#41	80 yds. [73.2m]

ATTACHMENT KEY:
— Napkin Holder Side/Bottom

C – Napkin Holder Bottom Side Piece
(cut 6) 5 x 13 holes

Whipstitch to B.

A – Napkin Holder Side Piece
(cut 2) 49 x 53 holes

Napkin Holder Assembly Illustration
(Pieces are shown in different colors for contrast; gray denotes wrong side.)

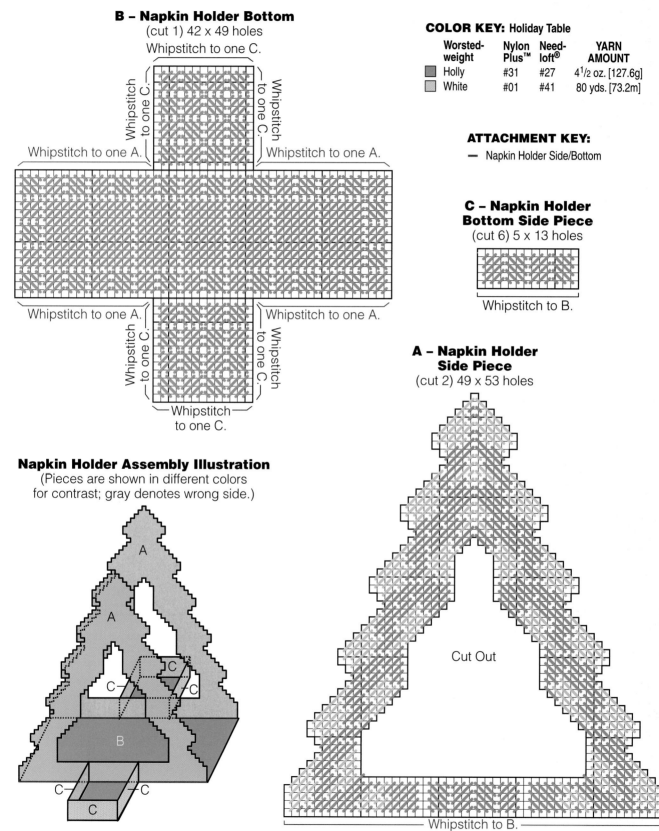

Cut Out

Whipstitch to B.

SANTA SNACKS

Designed by
Jeannette Osborne

Instructions on next page

SANTA SNACKS

(Photo on page 89.)

SIZES: Nut Holder is 6½" across x 5" tall [16.2cm x 12.7cm], not including side holder; each Small Container is 4¼" across x 4¾" tall [10.8cm x 12.1cm]; Medium Container is 3" across x 8" tall [7.6cm x 20.3cm]; Large Container is 3⅝" across x 9⅞" x tall [9.2cm x 25.1cm]. Measurements do not include beards, mustaches or pom-poms.

MATERIALS FOR SET: One 13½" x 22½" [34.3cm x 57.2cm] sheet of 7-count plastic canvas; Four standard-size sheets of clear and two of red 7-count plastic canvas; Three Darice® 4¼" [10.8cm] plastic canvas radial circles; one Darice® 9½" [24.1cm] plastic canvas circle; Fine-tooth comb; Hair spray; Craft glue or glue gun; Metallic cord (for amount see Color Key on page 93); Glitter yarn (for amount see Color Key) or use worsted-weight or plastic canvas yarn; Worsted-weight or plastic canvas yarn (for amounts see Color Key).

NOTES: Use Crossed Whipstitch and Crossed Overcast for Whipstitching and Overcasting, if desired.
Graphs on pages 92-95.

NUT HOLDER
CUTTING INSTRUCTIONS:
A: For nut holder side, cut one from large sheet 32 x 136 holes.
B: For nut holder lining pieces, from red, cut one 32 x 90 holes and one 32 x 43 holes (no graphs).
C: For nut holder bottom, cut away ten outer rows of holes from 9½" circle (no graph).
D: For nutcracker holder front, cut one from clear 23 x 25 holes.
E: For nutcracker holder back, cut one from clear 23 x 25 holes.
F: For nutcracker holder sides, cut two from clear 5 x 25 holes.
G: For nutcracker holder bottom, cut one from clear 5 x 23 holes.

STITCHING INSTRUCTIONS:
NOTE: B and C pieces are not worked.
1: Overlapping ends as indicated on graph and working through both thicknesses at overlap area to join, work A according to graph; using colors and stitches indicated, work D-G pieces according to graphs.
2: Using white and Modified Turkey Work (Leave 1½" [3.8m] loops in mustache area and ¾" [1.9m] loops in beard area.), embroider A as indicated.
3: With red, Whipstitch and assemble A-F pieces according to Nut Holder Assembly Diagram on page 92.
NOTE: Cut one 2-yd. [1.8m] and one 4" [10.2cm] length of white yarn.
4: For pom-pom, wrap 2-yd. strand around two fingers; using 4" strand, tie between fingers. Slip yarn off fingers and tighten knot; cut through loops. Glue pom-pom to A as indicated.
5: Cut through mustache and beard loops; comb to fray, trim and style as shown in photo or as desired. Lightly spray mustache and beard with hair spray.

CONTAINERS
CUTTING INSTRUCTIONS:
A: For small container sides, cut two from clear 31 x 90 holes.
B: For small container lining, cut one from red 31 x 86 holes (no graph).
C: For small container bottom, use one 4¼" circle (no graph).
D: For medium container side, cut one from clear 53 x 64 holes.
E: For medium container lining, cut one from red 53 x 59 holes (no graph).
F: For medium container bottom, cut away four outer rows of holes from one 4¼" circle (no graph).
G: For large container side, cut one from clear 64 x 70 holes.
H: For large container lid side, cut one from clear 17 x 77 holes.
I: For large container lid top, cut away two outer rows of holes from one 4¼" circle.

STITCHING INSTRUCTIONS:
NOTE: B, C, E, and F pieces are not worked.
1: Using colors (For lined A, substitute

black for royal on eyes, if desired.) and stitches indicated, work A, D, G, H (Overlap short edges of side pieces three holes and work through both thicknesses at overlap areas to join.) and I pieces according to graphs.

2: Using white and Modified Turkey Work (Leave 1½" [3.8cm] loops in mustache areas and ¾" [1.9cm] loops in beard areas.), embroider A, D and G pieces as indicated on graphs.

3: With red, Overcast edges of blue-eyed A.

4: For remaining Small Container, overlapping short edges of B three holes, insert B inside remaining A; with red, Whipstitch top edges of A and B pieces together. Whipstitch C to bottom edges of A and B pieces through all thicknesses.

5: For Medium Container, overlapping short edges of E three holes, insert E inside D; with red, Whipstitch top edges of D and E pieces together. Whipstitch F to bottom edges of D and E pieces through all thicknesses.

6: With red, Overcast edges of G. Whipstitch H and I pieces together, forming lid; Overcast unfinished edge of H.

NOTE: Cut four 2-yd. [1.8m] and four 4" [10.2cm] lengths of white yarn.

7: For each pom-pom (make four), follow Step 4 of Nut Holder. Glue one pom-pom to each A, D and I as indicated.

8: Cut through mustache and beard loops; comb to fray, trim and style as shown in photo or as desired. Lightly spray mustache and beard with hair spray.✢

Christmas Cooking

Just sit back, relax, and let Santa deliver all your Christmas goodies, including this mouth-watering, Honey Caramel Popcorn!

Recipe from the kitchen of Christmas Companion

Honey Caramel Popcorn

- 1 stick real butter (melted)
- ⅓ cup honey
- 1 cup of popcorn (unpopped)

Note: As the mixture cooks, pay close attention to the latter part of the cooking process. Once it reaches the boiling stage, the mixture cooks and goes to the firm ball stage rapidly. To test for firm ball stage, drizzle about ½ tsp. of the hot mixture into a cup of cool water. When the mixture forms a ball of caramel that retains its shape in the bottom of the cup of water, it has reached the firm ball stage.

Pop popcorn and fill a 9" x 13" baking dish. Put butter and honey in a four-cup glass measuring cup. Cook on high in microwave, stirring in one minute intervals until mixture is boiling. Then begin to stir in thirty-second intervals, until firm ball stage. Drizzle hot caramel over popped corn. Allow to cool, then cut into squares and enjoy!

SANTA SNACKS

(Instructions & photo on pages 89-91.)

Step 2:
Whipstitch D-G pieces together; Overcast unfinished edges.

Nut Holder Assembly Diagram
(Pieces are shown in different colors for contrast.)

Step 1:
Overlapping ends of B pieces three holes and inserting lining into A, Whipstitch top edges of A and B pieces together; Whipstitch C to bottom edges of A and B pieces through all thicknesses.

B – 32 x 43 Holes
3 Hole Overlap
3 Hole Overlap
C
B – 32 x 90 Holes
A

Step 3:
Glue nutcracker holder to nut holder.

Nutcracker Holder
Nut Holder

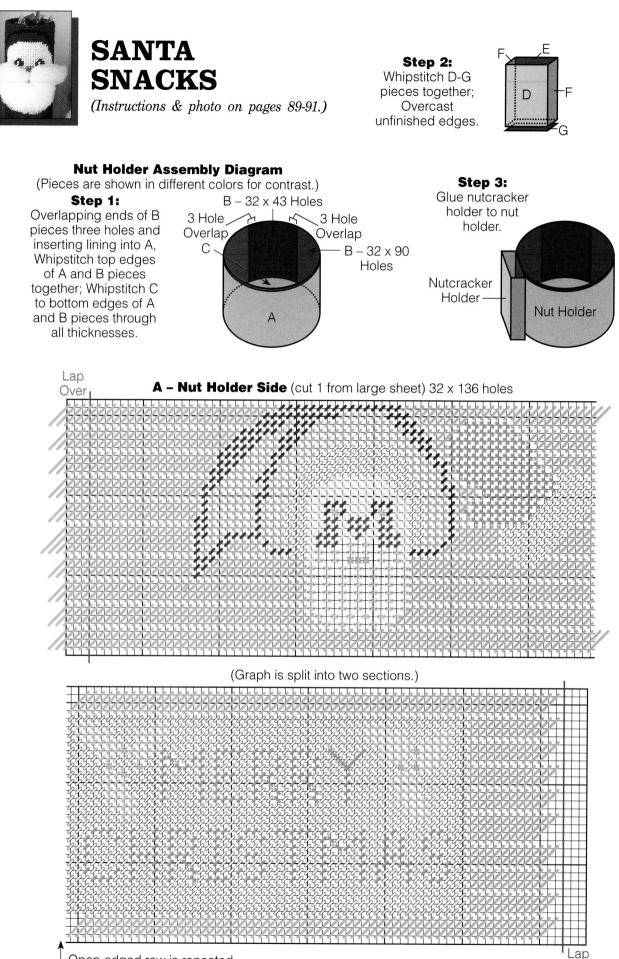

A – Nut Holder Side (cut 1 from large sheet) 32 x 136 holes

Lap Over

(Graph is split into two sections.)

Open-edged row is repeated.

Lap Under

COLOR KEY: Santa Snacks

Metallic cord			AMOUNT
■ Gold			2 yds. [1.8m]

Glitter yarn			AMOUNT
▨ White			50 yds. [45.7m]

Worsted-weight	Nylon Plus™	Need-loft®	YARN AMOUNT
▨ Red	#20	#01	7 oz. [198.5g]
▨ White	#01	#41	3³/4 oz. [106.3g]
▨ Forest	#32	#29	50 yds. [45.7m]
▨ Violet	#49	#04	19 yds. [17.4m]
▨ Holly	#31	#27	17 yds. [15.5m]
■ Black	#02	#00	12 yds. [11m]
▨ Coral	#14	#66	12 yds. [11m]
▨ Lavender	#12	#05	10 yds. [9.1m]
▨ Royal	#09	#32	4 yds. [3.7m]
▨ Yellow	#26	#57	4 yds. [3.7m]

STITCH KEY:

- ∽ Modified Turkey Work
- ◆ Pom-Pom Placement

D – Nutcracker Holder Front
(cut 1 from clear)
23 x 25 holes

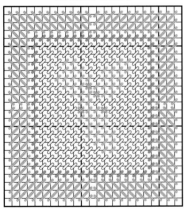

F – Nutcracker Holder Side
(cut 2 from clear)
5 x 25 holes

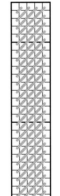

E – Nutcracker Holder Back
(cut 1 from clear)
23 x 25 holes

G – Nutcracker Holder Bottom
(cut 1 from clear)
5 x 23 holes

A – Small Container Side (cut 2 from clear) 31 x 90 holes

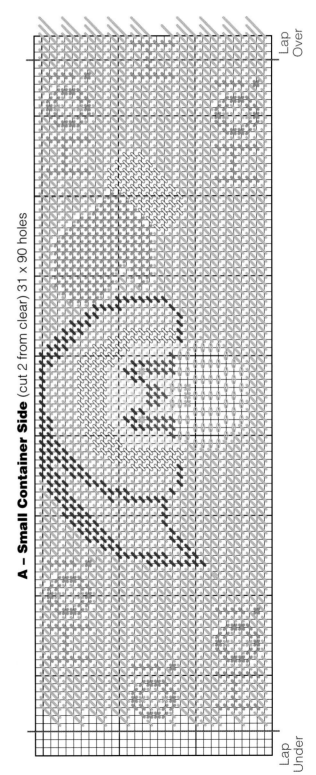

Lap Over

Lap Under

SANTA SNACKS

(Instructions & photo on pages 89-91.)

D – Medium Container Side (cut 1 from clear) 53 x 64 holes

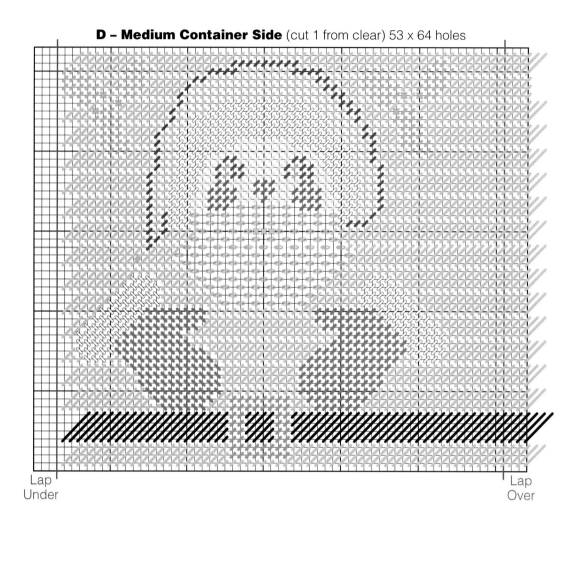

Lap
Under

Lap
Over

H – Large Container Lid Side (cut 1 from clear) 17 x 77 holes

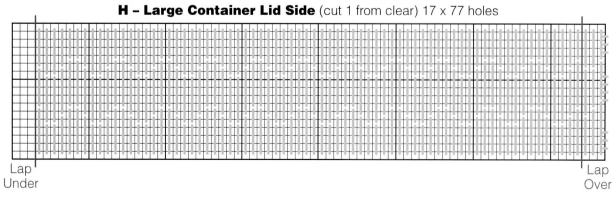

Lap
Under

Lap
Over

Tasty Creations For The Cook

I – Large Container Lid Top
(cut 1 from 4¹/4" circle)
Cut away gray area.

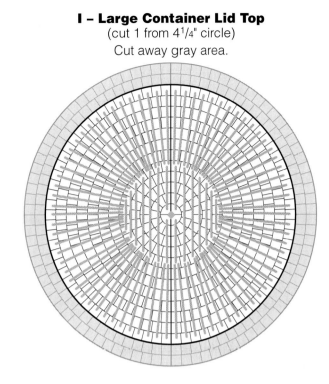

G – Large Container Side (cut 1 from clear) 64 x 70 holes

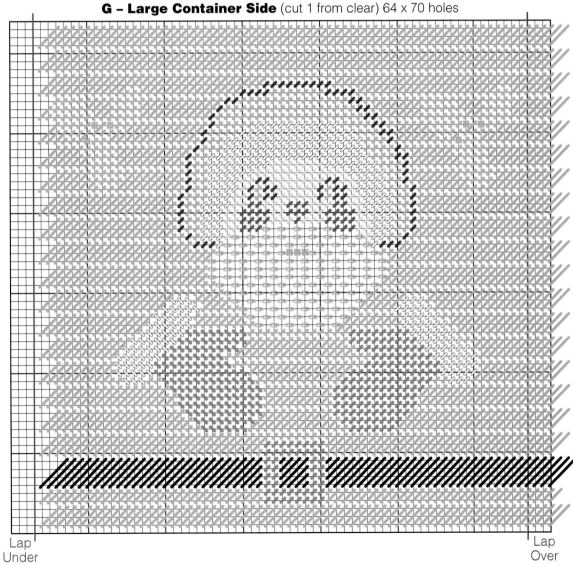

Lap Under

Lap Over

Day Brighteners for your Co-Workers

Chapter Five

Designed by
Virginia Volk

Tip

Use these signs as Christmas cards for your co-workers, by attaching a signed card to the back.

SIZES: Ho Ho Ho is 3¾" x 12" [9.5cm 30.5cm]; Santa and Noel are 3¾" x 10¾" [9.5cm x 27.3cm] not including lace.

MATERIALS: Three sheets of 7-count plastic canvas; 2½ yds. [2.3m] red 4mm pearl strand; 1⅔ yds. [1.8m] red ¼" [6mm] picot-edged satin ribbon; 1 yd. [0.9m] white ¼" [6mm] picot-edged satin ribbon, ⅔ yd. [0.6m] each gold and green ¼" [6mm] picot-edged satin ribbon; ½ yd. [0.5m] green ⅛" [3mm] satin ribbon; Four small red ribbon roses; Two white ½" [6mm] silk roses with greenery; 2 yds. [1.8m] red and green 1" [2.5cm] pre-gathered lace; 1 yd. [0.9m] red 1¼" [3.2cm] pre-gathered lace; Craft glue or glue gun; Medium metallic braid or metallic cord (for amount see Color Key on page 100); Six-strand embroidery floss (for amounts see Color Key); Worsted-weight or plastic canvas yarn (for amounts see Color Key).

CUTTING INSTRUCTIONS:
NOTE: Graphs on page 100.
A: For Ho Ho Ho front and backing, cut two (one for front and one for backing) 22 x 79 holes.
B: For Noel front and backing, cut two (one for front and one for backing) 24 x 71 holes.
C: For Santa front and backing, cut two (one for front and one for backing) 24 x 71 holes.
D: For hangers, cut three according to graph.

STITCHING INSTRUCTIONS:
NOTE: Backings are not worked.
1: Using colors and stitches indicated, work front A-C pieces according to graphs.
2: Using metallic braid, yarn (Separate into individual plies, if desired.) and six strands floss in colors and embroidery stitches indicated, embroider detail as indicated on graphs.

3: Center one D piece eight holes from top of each backing; using white and Continental Stitch, work through both thicknesses as one piece according to D graph.
4: Holding one backing to wrong side of each front, with white, Whipstitch together.
5: Glue pearl stand around front edges and lace around back edges of each piece (see photo).
NOTE: Cut red ribbon into one 24" [61cm] and two 18" [45.7cm] lengths; cut white ribbon into two 18" [45.7cm] lengths.
6: For Ho Ho Ho, holding one 24" red ribbon and gold and green picot ribbons together, tie into a triple-loop bow with 2" [5.1cm] loops; glue two ribbon roses to center. Glue bow to bottom (see photo).
7: For Noel, holding one red 18", one white 18" and narrow green ribbons together, tie into a bow with 1½" [3.8cm] loops as in Step 6; glue one ribbon rose and one white rose to center. Glue bow to top corner (see photo).
8: For Santa, holding remaining red and white ribbons together, tie into a bow with 1½" [3.8cm] loops as in Step 6; glue remaining roses to center. Glue bow to top corner (see photo).✣

Gift Idea
Make two each of the Santa and Noel signs and attach the sides of all four of them to make a tall, rectangular box. Then, make a bottom for the box and give it to a co-worker to put pencils, pens, scissors and other office supplies in.

SIGNS OF CHRISTMAS

(Instructions & photo on pages 98 & 99.)

A – Ho Ho Ho Front & Backing
(cut 1 each) 22 x 79 holes

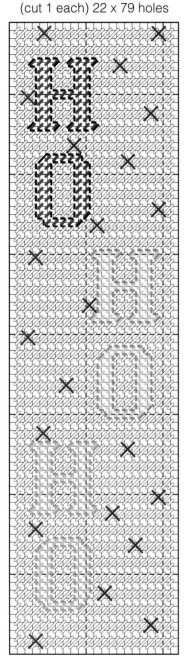

B – Noel Front & Backing
(cut 1 each) 24 x 71 holes

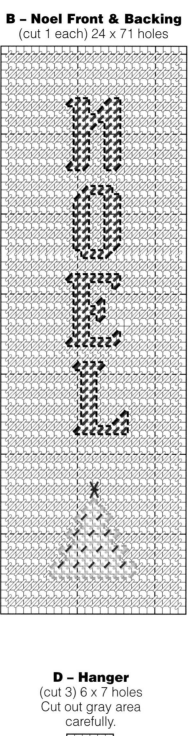

C – Santa Front & Backing
(cut 1 each) 24 x 71 holes

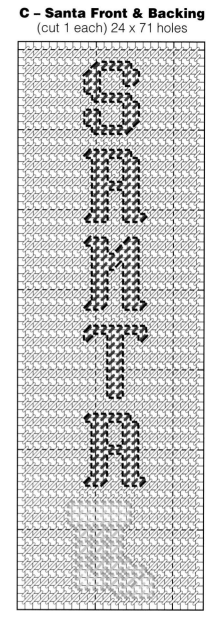

D – Hanger
(cut 3) 6 x 7 holes
Cut out gray area
carefully.

COLOR KEY: Signs Of Christmas

Metallic braid or cord			AMOUNT
■ Gold			3 yds. [2.7m]

Embroidery floss			AMOUNT
▨ Dk. Yellow			3 yds. [2.7m]

Worsted-weight	Nylon Plus™	Need-loft®	YARN AMOUNT
▨ White	#01	#41	75 yds. [68.6m]
■ Xmas Red	#19	#02	8 yds. [7.3m]
▨ Holly	#31	#27	6 yds. [5.5m]
■ Red	#20	#01	6 yds. [5.5m]
▨ Bt. Yellow	–	#63	4 yds. [3.7m]
▨ Xmas Green	#58	#28	4 yds. [3.7m]

STITCH KEY:
— Backstitch/Straight
✕ Cross Stitch

HOME SWEET OFFICE

(Photo on page 101.)

SIZE: 10½" x 13½" [26.7cm x 34.3cm], not including trims.

MATERIALS: One sheet of 7-count plastic canvas; ¼ yd. [0.2m] coordinating color 45" [114.3cm] poly-cotton fabric; 2½ yds. [2.3m] gold ³⁄₁₆" [5mm] twisted cord; Two gold 2" [5.1cm] tassels; ¼ yd. [6mm] pink ⅛" [3mm] satin ribbon; Sewing needle and matching color thread; Craft glue or glue gun; Six-strand embroidery floss (for amount see Color Key); Worsted-weight or plastic canvas yarn (for amounts see Color Key).

CUTTING INSTRUCTIONS:

For Home Sweet Office, use one 70- x 90-hole sheet.

STITCHING INSTRUCTIONS:

1: Using colors and stitches indicated, work piece according to graph; fill in uncoded areas using royal dark and Continental Stitch. With gold, Overcast unfinished edges.

2: Using yarn (Separate into individual plies, if desired.) and one strand floss in colors and embroidery stitches indicated,

Gift Idea

Attach a dry-erase calendar to the bottom of the sign, then give it to your friend so he can mark his important appointments, while being reminded of how home-like the office is.

Tassel Assembly Illustration

— Cord

— Gold Thread

Tassel —

Tip

Display a jolly reminder of where the heart so often is, by hanging this sign near your desk. Attach a plastic hook on the bottom center of the sign to hang your gloves, hat or umbrella from. How about adding a collage made from photos of your family to hang from this sign to make your office really feel like home.

COLOR KEY: Home Sweet Office

	Embroidery floss			AMOUNT
■	White			½ yd. [0.5m]

	Worsted-weight	Nylon Plus™	Need-loft®	YARN AMOUNT
☐	Royal Dark	#07	#48	40 yds. [36.6m]
■	Gold	#27	#17	18 yds. [15.5m]
■	Gray	#23	#38	8 yds. [7.3m]
■	Eggshell	#24	#39	7 yds. [6.4m]
■	Silver	–	#37	6 yds. [5.5m]
■	Xmas Red	#19	#02	4 yds. [3.7m]
■	Baby Blue	#05	#36	3 yds. [2.7m]
■	Black	#02	#00	2 yds. [1.8m]
▨	Lemon	#25	#20	2 yds. [1.8m]
☐	Sail Blue	#04	#35	2 yds. [1.8m]
■	Watermelon	#54	#55	2 yds. [1.8m]
■	Xmas Green	#58	#28	2 yds. [1.8m]
■	Mermaid Green	#37	#53	1½ yds. [1.4m]
■	Pumpkin	#50	#12	1½ yds. [1.4m]
■	Violet	#49	#04	1½ yds. [1.4m]
☐	Pink	#11	#07	1 yd. [0.9m]
■	Tan	#33	#18	1 yd. [0.9m]
▨	White	#01	#41	1 yd. [0.9m]

STITCH KEY:
- — Backstitch/Straight
- ✕ Cross
- ◆ Bow Placement

embroider detail as indicated on graph.

3: Trimming to fit and starting at center bottom, glue twisted cord to outer edges; cut remaining cord in half.

4: Cut two 4" x 45" [10.2cm x 114.3cm] strips of fabric. Using ½" [13mm] seams, sew short ends right sides together; fold in half lengthwise and press wrong sides together. Sew a line of gathering stitches ½" [13mm] from raw edges; gather threads to fit around edges of wall hanging. Glue raw edges around back edges of piece.

5: With gold thread, attach one tassel to one end of each cord according to Tassel Attachment Illustration; glue opposite ends to top corners on wrong side. Tie tassel ends into a bow for hanger.

6: Tie ribbon into a bow; trim ends as desired. Glue bow to piece as indicated.✣

Home Sweet Office (use 70- x 90-hole sheet)

Gift Idea

Fill this whimsical mug with colored pens, Christmas sticky notes, colorful paper clips, candy or personalized office supplies and present it to a friend. Or you can give it filled with some chocolates and gourmet coffee.

SIZE: 3" x 7¾" x 9" tall [7.6cm x 19.7cm x 22.9cm].

MATERIALS: 1¼ sheets of clear and ¼ sheet of dk. green 7-count plastic canvas; One 3" [7.6cm] plastic canvas radial circle; One tan chenille stem; Craft glue or glue gun; Metallic cord (for amount see Color Key); Worsted-weight or plastic canvas yarn (for amounts see Color Key).

CUTTING INSTRUCTIONS:

NOTES: Use green for C and clear canvas for remaining pieces.

Graphs continued on page 106.

A: For mug side, cut one 25 x 63 holes.

B: For mug bottom, use 3" circle (no graph).

C: For mug liner, cut one from green 24 x 57 holes (no graph).

D: For mug handle pieces, cut three according to graph.

E: For reindeer front and back, cut one

each according to graphs.

F: For reindeer front and back arms, cut one each according to graphs.

G: For reindeer front and back legs, cut one each according to graphs.

H: For reindeer tail, cut one according to graph.

STITCHING INSTRUCTIONS:

NOTES: B, C and one D pieces are not worked.

1: Using colors and stitches indicated, work A (overlap holes at ends as indicated on graph and work through both thicknesses at overlap area to join), two D (one on opposite side of canvas) and E-H pieces according to graphs.

2: With matching colors, Overcast edges of F-H pieces.

3: Using yarn (Separate into individual plies, if desired.) in colors and embroidery stitches indicated, embroider detail on A and E-G pieces as indicated.

4: Shape chenille stem into antlers according to Antler Assembly Illustration. For reindeer, holding antlers between front and back as indicated, with camel for ears and chest and with matching colors, Whipstitch E pieces wrong sides together as indicated; Whipstitch reindeer to A as indicated.

5: For handle, holding worked D pieces wrong sides together with unworked piece between, with cord, Whipstitch together through all thicknesses as indicated; Whipstitch handle to A as indicated.

6: With cord, Whipstitch A and B pieces together; Overcast top edge. For liner, overlapping ends of C three holes, using Xmas green and Long Stitch, work through both thicknesses at overlap area to join. Set liner inside mug.

7: Matching bottom edges, glue G pieces to reindeer and mug; glue H to reindeer as indicated and F pieces to reindeer and mug as shown in photo.✚

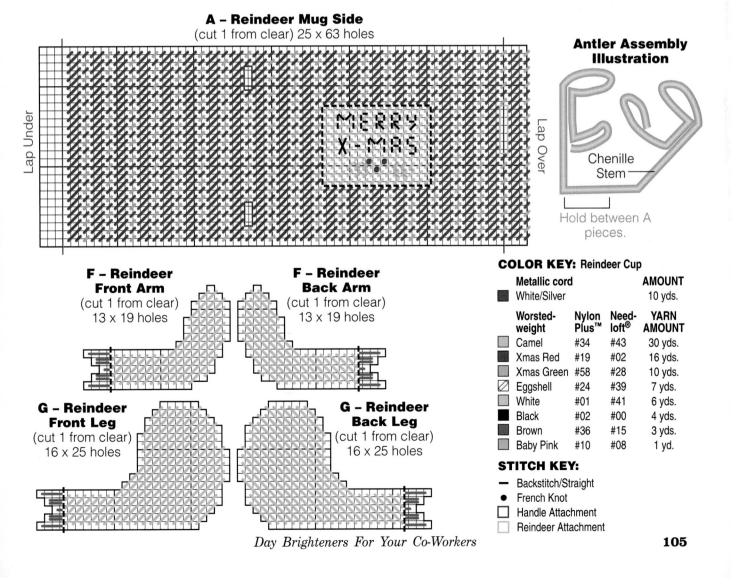

A – Reindeer Mug Side
(cut 1 from clear) 25 x 63 holes

Lap Under

Lap Over

MERRY X-MAS

Antler Assembly Illustration

Chenille Stem

Hold between A pieces.

F – Reindeer Front Arm
(cut 1 from clear)
13 x 19 holes

F – Reindeer Back Arm
(cut 1 from clear)
13 x 19 holes

G – Reindeer Front Leg
(cut 1 from clear)
16 x 25 holes

G – Reindeer Back Leg
(cut 1 from clear)
16 x 25 holes

COLOR KEY: Reindeer Cup

Metallic cord			AMOUNT
White/Silver			10 yds.

Worsted-weight	Nylon Plus™	Need-loft®	YARN AMOUNT
Camel	#34	#43	30 yds.
Xmas Red	#19	#02	16 yds.
Xmas Green	#58	#28	10 yds.
Eggshell	#24	#39	7 yds.
White	#01	#41	6 yds.
Black	#02	#00	4 yds.
Brown	#36	#15	3 yds.
Baby Pink	#10	#08	1 yd.

STITCH KEY:
— Backstitch/Straight
● French Knot
☐ Handle Attachment
☐ Reindeer Attachment

Day Brighteners For Your Co-Workers

REINDEER CUP

(Instructions & photo on pages 104 & 105.)

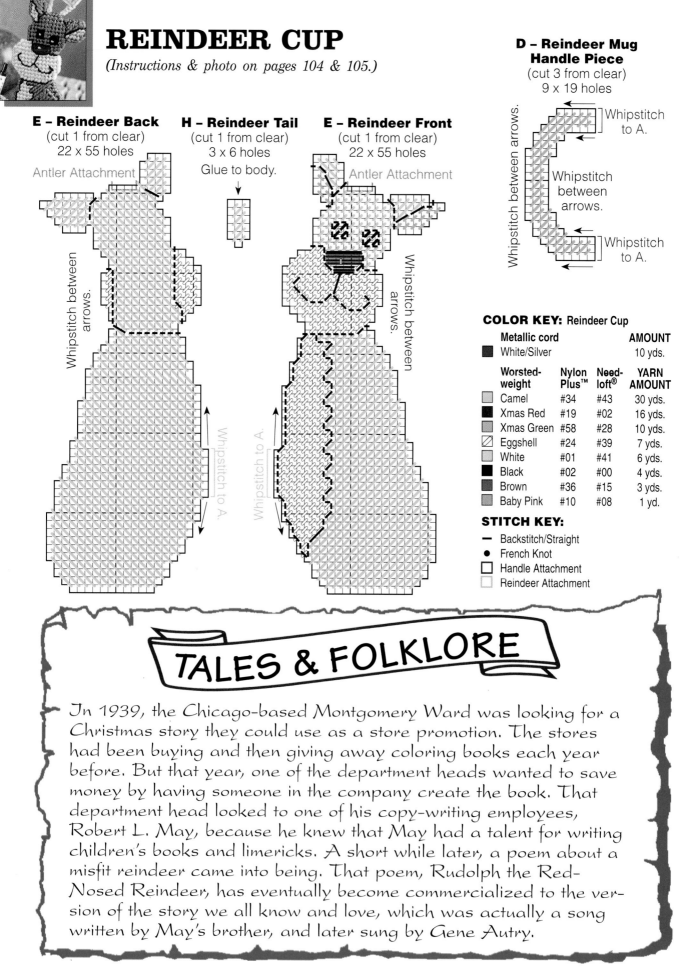

D – Reindeer Mug Handle Piece
(cut 3 from clear)
9 x 19 holes

Whipstitch between arrows.

Whipstitch to A.

Whipstitch between arrows.

Whipstitch to A.

E – Reindeer Back
(cut 1 from clear)
22 x 55 holes

Antler Attachment

Whipstitch between arrows.

H – Reindeer Tail
(cut 1 from clear)
3 x 6 holes
Glue to body.

E – Reindeer Front
(cut 1 from clear)
22 x 55 holes

Antler Attachment

Whipstitch between arrows.

Whipstitch to A.

Whipstitch to A.

COLOR KEY: Reindeer Cup

	Metallic cord			AMOUNT
■	White/Silver			10 yds.

	Worsted-weight	Nylon Plus™	Need-loft®	YARN AMOUNT
	Camel	#34	#43	30 yds.
	Xmas Red	#19	#02	16 yds.
	Xmas Green	#58	#28	10 yds.
	Eggshell	#24	#39	7 yds.
	White	#01	#41	6 yds.
	Black	#02	#00	4 yds.
	Brown	#36	#15	3 yds.
	Baby Pink	#10	#08	1 yd.

STITCH KEY:
— Backstitch/Straight
● French Knot
▫ Handle Attachment
▫ Reindeer Attachment

TALES & FOLKLORE

In 1939, the Chicago-based Montgomery Ward was looking for a Christmas story they could use as a store promotion. The stores had been buying and then giving away coloring books each year before. But that year, one of the department heads wanted to save money by having someone in the company create the book. That department head looked to one of his copy-writing employees, Robert L. May, because he knew that May had a talent for writing children's books and limericks. A short while later, a poem about a misfit reindeer came into being. That poem, Rudolph the Red-Nosed Reindeer, has eventually become commercialized to the version of the story we all know and love, which was actually a song written by May's brother, and later sung by Gene Autry.

HOLIDAY SHELF SITTERS

Designed by Nancy Marshall

Instructions on next page

Tip

Cheer up a work-laden co-worker by tucking one of these into unsuspecting office spaces such as the printer room, by the fax machine, the water cooler, someone's desk, the coat rack or in the break room.

107

HOLIDAY SHELF SITTERS

(Photo on page 107.)

SIZES: Santa is 4¾" x 7½" [12.1cm x 19cm]; Elf is 4¾" x 7" [12.1cm x 17.8cm]; Snowman is 5" x 6¾" [12.7 x 17.1cm].

MATERIALS: 1½ sheets of 7-count plastic canvas; ⅓ yd. [0.3m] Christmas plaid ⅜" [10mm] ribbon; One red ½" [13mm] pom-pom; Two green 18mm holly leaf acrylic stones; One red 9mm round acrylic stone; Craft glue or glue gun; Six-strand embroidery floss (for amounts see Color Key); Worsted-weight or plastic canvas yarn (for amounts see Color Key).

CUTTING INSTRUCTIONS:

A: For Santa front and backing, cut two (one for front and one for backing) according to graph.

B: For Santa arms, cut two according to graph.

C: For Santa legs, cut one according to graph.

D: For Elf front and backing, cut two (one for front and one for backing) according to graph.

E: For Elf arms, cut two according to graph.

F: For Elf legs, cut one according to graph.

G: For Snowman front and backing, cut two (one for front and one for backing) according to graph.

H: For Snowman arms, cut two according to graph.

I: For Snowman legs, cut one according to graph.

J: For stands, cut three 7 x 13 holes (no graph).

STITCHING INSTRUCTIONS:

NOTE: Backings A, D and G and J pieces are not worked.

1: Using colors and stitches indicated, work A-H (one B, one E and one H piece on opposite side of canvas) pieces according to graphs; fill in uncoded areas using Xmas red and Continental Stitch. With matching colors, Overcast indicated edges of B, E and H pieces and edges of C, F and I pieces.

2: Using six strands floss in colors and embroidery stitches indicated, embroider detail on A, C, D, F, G and I pieces as indicated on graphs.

3: Whipstitch and assemble corresponding pieces according to Shelf Sitter Assembly Diagram.

NOTE: Cut one 1½" [3.8cm] length of white yarn; tie a knot in center of strand and fray each end for mustache.

4: Glue pom-pom to Santa as indicated for nose; glue mustache under pom-pom (see photo). Tie ribbon around Snowman's neck and stones to hat as shown.‡

A – Santa Front & Backing
(cut 1 each) 17 x 38 holes

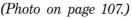

B – Santa Arm
(cut 2) 11 x 16 holes

Overcast between arrows.

C – Santa Legs
(cut 1) 17 x 21 holes

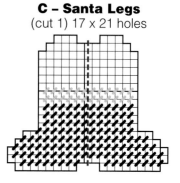

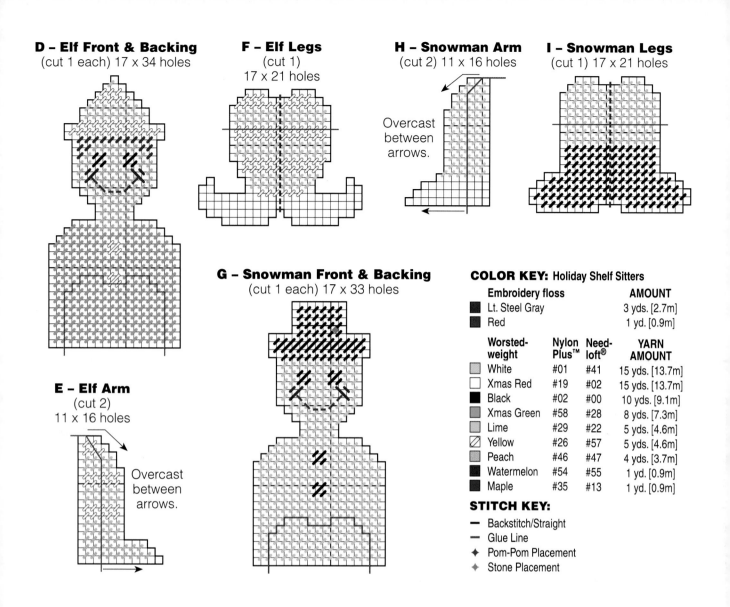

D – Elf Front & Backing
(cut 1 each) 17 x 34 holes

F – Elf Legs
(cut 1)
17 x 21 holes

H – Snowman Arm
(cut 2) 11 x 16 holes

Overcast between arrows.

I – Snowman Legs
(cut 1) 17 x 21 holes

E – Elf Arm
(cut 2)
11 x 16 holes

Overcast between arrows.

G – Snowman Front & Backing
(cut 1 each) 17 x 33 holes

COLOR KEY: Holiday Shelf Sitters

Embroidery floss			AMOUNT
Lt. Steel Gray			3 yds. [2.7m]
Red			1 yd. [0.9m]

Worsted-weight	Nylon Plus™	Need-loft®	YARN AMOUNT
White	#01	#41	15 yds. [13.7m]
Xmas Red	#19	#02	15 yds. [13.7m]
Black	#02	#00	10 yds. [9.1m]
Xmas Green	#58	#28	8 yds. [7.3m]
Lime	#29	#22	5 yds. [4.6m]
Yellow	#26	#57	5 yds. [4.6m]
Peach	#46	#47	4 yds. [3.7m]
Watermelon	#54	#55	1 yd. [0.9m]
Maple	#35	#13	1 yd. [0.9m]

STITCH KEY:
— Backstitch/Straight
— Glue Line
✦ Pom-Pom Placement
✦ Stone Placement

Shelf Sitter Assembly Diagram
(Pieces are shown in different colors for contrast; gray denotes wrong side.)

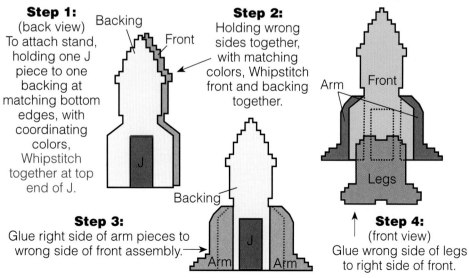

Step 1:
(back view)
To attach stand, holding one J piece to one backing at matching bottom edges, with coordinating colors, Whipstitch together at top end of J.

Step 2:
Holding wrong sides together, with matching colors, Whipstitch front and backing together.

Step 3:
Glue right side of arm pieces to wrong side of front assembly.

Step 4:
(front view)
Glue wrong side of legs to right side of front.

MERRY ELF

Designed by Celia Lange Designs

Tip

Use this delightful guy as a friendly reminder of rotating office responsibilities. This technique seems to convey the unpleasant news in a more cheerful way.

SIZE: 2¼" x 6" x 11¼" tall [5.7cm x 15.2cm x 28.6cm].

MATERIALS: Two sheets of 7-count plastic canvas; Two sheets of natural tissue paper; One red ³⁄₁₆" [5mm] round button; Eight gold ¼" [6mm] round buttons; One yellow ¾" [19mm] star shank button; Two 10mm wiggle eyes; One gold 6mm jingle bell; 6" [15.2cm] length of auburn doll hair; One toothpick; Sewing needle and matching color thread; Craft glue or glue gun; Heavy metallic braid or metallic cord (for amount see Color Key on page 112); #3 pearl cotton or six-strand embroidery floss (for amount see Color Key); Worsted-weight or plastic canvas yarn (for amounts see Color Key).

CUTTING INSTRUCTIONS:
NOTE: Graphs on page 112.
A: For box front, cut one 29 x 29 holes.

B: For box back, cut one 29 x 29 holes.
C: For box sides, cut two 14 x 29 holes.
D: For box bottom, cut one 14 x 29 holes (no graph).
E: For elf front and back, cut two (one for front and one for back) according to graph.
F: For elf side, cut two according to graph.
G: For head front and back, cut two (one for front and one for back) according to graph.
H: For cap front and back, cut two (one for front and one for back) according to graph.
I: For left arm front and back, cut two (one for front and one for back) according to graph.
J: For right arm front and back, cut two (one for front and one for back) according to graph.
K: For hands, cut two according to graph.
L: For ears, cut two according to graph.

STITCHING INSTRUCTIONS:

1: Using colors and stitches indicated, work A-C, E-G and H-L (one each on opposite side of canvas) pieces according to graphs; using burgundy and Continental Stitch, work D. With sandstone, Overcast edges of K and L pieces; with burgundy, Overcast bottom edges of H pieces as indicated on graph.

2: Using metallic braid or cord and pearl cotton or six strands floss in colors and embroidery stitches indicated, embroider detail on A, C, one E for front and one G piece for front as indicated.

3: With sandstone, Whipstitch A-D pieces together to form box; Overcast edges.

4: With teal blue, holding corresponding pieces wrong sides together, Whipstitch H-J pieces together as indicated; Overcast unfinished edges of arms. Holding G pieces wrong sides together, with sandstone, Whipstitch together as indicated; Overcast unfinished edges.

5: Whipstitch and assemble E-K pieces and hair according to Elf Assembly Diagram on page 112.

6: Center Elf inside box and glue to secure; stuff tissue paper in each side (see photo).

7: Glue ears as indicated to back of head. Glue bell, eyes and buttons to Elf as indicated; glue star button to one end of toothpick and toothpick to right hand as shown.‡

Heartwarming Story

Fran Rohus, Design Director for the Needlecraft Shop, sewed a teddy bear when she was just a little girl, completely unaware of what would happen to him later. When she began working here, she turned her bear into the "bearer" of kitchen duty appointments. Over the years, recipients of this doll have taken out their frustrations on him and have shown their creative talents through him. You see, he has a split personality. One of his sides is sweet, while the other is a bit capricious. On his naughty side, he has now lost one eye, acquired a tattoo and an earring, while his innocent side has been embellished with an apron, a hair bow and eyelashes. He was even kidnapped once by a disenchanted kitchen cleaner. Fortunately, he was later returned without being held for ransom. Now, the bear has become more of a contest to see how naughty or nice his two faces can be. But, we just enjoy passing him around to see the reaction of the next person who gets him tucked into her in-box. — Kim Votaw

MERRY ELF

(Instructions & photo on pages 110 & 111.)

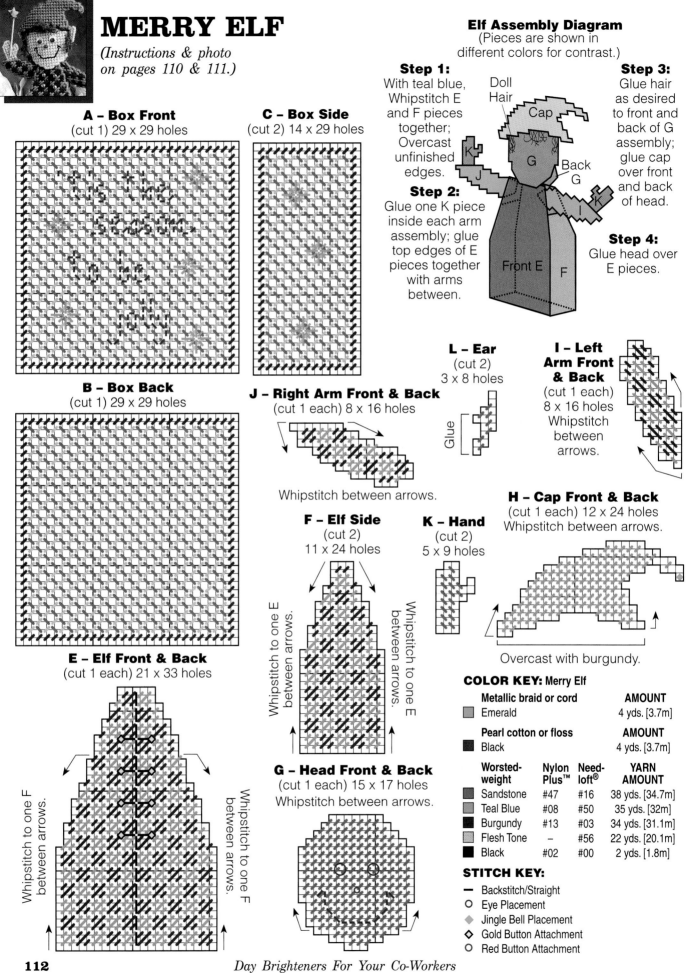

Elf Assembly Diagram
(Pieces are shown in different colors for contrast.)

Step 1:
With teal blue, Whipstitch E and F pieces together; Overcast unfinished edges.

Doll Hair

Cap

K

J

G

Back G

K

I

Step 3:
Glue hair as desired to front and back of G assembly; glue cap over front and back of head.

Step 2:
Glue one K piece inside each arm assembly; glue top edges of E pieces together with arms between.

Step 4:
Glue head over E pieces.

Front E   F

A – Box Front
(cut 1) 29 x 29 holes

C – Box Side
(cut 2) 14 x 29 holes

B – Box Back
(cut 1) 29 x 29 holes

J – Right Arm Front & Back
(cut 1 each) 8 x 16 holes

Whipstitch between arrows.

L – Ear
(cut 2)
3 x 8 holes

Glue

I – Left Arm Front & Back
(cut 1 each)
8 x 16 holes
Whipstitch between arrows.

F – Elf Side
(cut 2)
11 x 24 holes

Whipstitch to one E between arrows.

Whipstitch to one E between arrows.

K – Hand
(cut 2)
5 x 9 holes

H – Cap Front & Back
(cut 1 each) 12 x 24 holes
Whipstitch between arrows.

Overcast with burgundy.

E – Elf Front & Back
(cut 1 each) 21 x 33 holes

Whipstitch to one F between arrows.

Whipstitch to one F between arrows.

G – Head Front & Back
(cut 1 each) 15 x 17 holes
Whipstitch between arrows.

COLOR KEY: Merry Elf

Metallic braid or cord			AMOUNT
Emerald			4 yds. [3.7m]
Pearl cotton or floss			**AMOUNT**
Black			4 yds. [3.7m]

Worsted-weight	Nylon Plus™	Need-loft®	YARN AMOUNT
Sandstone	#47	#16	38 yds. [34.7m]
Teal Blue	#08	#50	35 yds. [32m]
Burgundy	#13	#03	34 yds. [31.1m]
Flesh Tone	–	#56	22 yds. [20.1m]
Black	#02	#00	2 yds. [1.8m]

STITCH KEY:
- — Backstitch/Straight
- O Eye Placement
- ◆ Jingle Bell Placement
- ◇ Gold Button Attachment
- O Red Button Attachment

WELCOME PENGUIN

*Designed by
Michele Wilcox*

Instructions on next page

WELCOME PENGUIN

(Photo on page 113.)

SIZE: 10½" x 13½" [26.7cm x 34.3cm].

MATERIALS: Two sheets of 7-count plastic canvas; #3 pearl cotton or six-strand embroidery floss (for amount see Color Key); Worsted-weight or plastic canvas yarn (for amounts see Color Key).

CUTTING INSTRUCTIONS:
For Welcome front and backing, use two (one for front and one for backing) 70- x 90-hole sheets.

STITCHING INSTRUCTIONS:
NOTE: Backing is not worked.
1: Using colors and stitches indicated, work one piece for front according to graph; fill in uncoded areas using white and Continental Stitch.
2: Using pearl cotton or six strands floss and French Knot, embroider eyes as indicated on graph.
3: Holding backing to wrong side of front, with royal, Whipstitch together.
4: Hang as desired.✣

Tip

Welcome everyone inside from the cold weather by hanging this cheerful sign on the bulletin board or office door. Try making a thought-for-the-day board for your office by using this Winter Welcome as a topper for a small-sized, dry-erase board. Then, donate the board to your break room and begin your own tradition of inspiring displays.

COLOR KEY: Welcome Penguin

Pearl cotton or floss			AMOUNT
Med. Blue			½ yd. [0.5m]

Worsted-weight	Nylon Plus™	Need-loft®	YARN AMOUNT
White	#01	#41	55 yds. [50.3m]
Royal	#09	#32	22 yds. [20.1m]
Black	#02	#00	18 yds. [16.5m]
Red	#20	#01	10 yds. [9.1m]
Rose	#52	#06	9 yds. [8.2m]
Pewter	#40	#65	5 yds. [4.6m]
Tangerine	#15	#11	5 yds. [4.6m]
Xmas Green	#58	#28	5 yds. [4.6m]
Yellow	#26	#57	5 yds. [4.6m]

STITCH KEY:
● French Knot

Heartwarming Story

To inspire everyone in our offices, we have a thought-for-the-day board on which we write encouraging quotes, proverbs or other sayings. What is more enjoyable about our board is that we can hardly walk by it without embellishing the quote with decorative drawings. That makes the sayings mean more to each of us, while giving us something profound to think of during the day. – Salway Sabri

Welcome Front (use 70- x 90-hole sheet)

Simple Pleasures for Special People

Chapter Six

SWEET FACE COASTERS

Designed by Joyce Keklock

Gift Idea

These cute and heartwarming gingerbread face coasters can add life to your holiday festivities. Stitch one and attach it to a plain mug filled with hot drink packets, then present it to your favorite professional helping hand, such as a nurse, doctor, optometrist or dentist.

SIZES: Each Coaster is 4" across [10.2cm].

MATERIALS: One sheet of 7-count plastic canvas; 1 yd. [0.9m] green ¼" [6mm] satin ribbon; Craft glue or glue gun; Six-strand embroidery floss (for amount see Color Key); Worsted-weight or plastic canvas yarn (for amounts see Color Key).

CUTTING INSTRUCTIONS:

For Coasters, cut four according to graph.

STITCHING INSTRUCTIONS:

1: Using colors indicated (fill in uncoded areas using maple) and Continental Stitch, work pieces according to graph; with white, Overcast edges.

2: Using yarn (Separate into individual plies, if desired.) and six strands floss in colors indicated and Backstitch, embroider detail on each piece as indicated on graph.

NOTE: Cut ribbon in four equal lengths; tie each strand into a bow.

3: Glue one bow to each Coaster as indicated.‡

Sweet Face Coaster
(cut 4) 25 x 25 holes

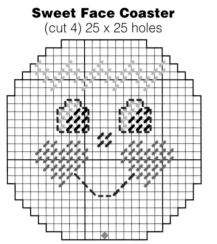

COLOR KEY: Sweet Face Coasters

Embroidery floss			AMOUNT
■ Black			½ yd. [0.5m]

Worsted-weight	Nylon Plus™	Need-loft®	YARN AMOUNT
☐ Maple	#35	#13	25 yds. [22.9m]
☐ White	#01	#41	12 yds. [11m]
■ Pink	#11	#07	6 yds. [5.5m]
■ Xmas Red	#19	#02	3 yds. [2.7m]
■ Black	#02	#00	3 yds. [2.7m]

STITCH KEY:

— Backstitch/Straight

◆ Bow Placement

Heartwarming Story

Gingerbread people and houses touch the imaginations of young and old alike. I've had the pleasure of experiencing annual gingerbread house shows put on to raise funds for our school. Sponsors from all over town (such as the electrician, carpenter, etc.) pitched in to make it an incredible holiday spectacle. Each year, their skills and creativity dazzled on-lookers. One year, they made Cinderella's castle; another year, Hansel and Gretle, and many, many others followed. The whole town came to see the lights gleam and the candies sparkle, smell the tempting aroma and experience a whole new world awakening before its very eyes. Everyone especially longed to see the costumed gingerbread people associated with the theme. With their smiles and various expressions, these gingerbread folks made a permanent impression in my heart. - Kim Votaw

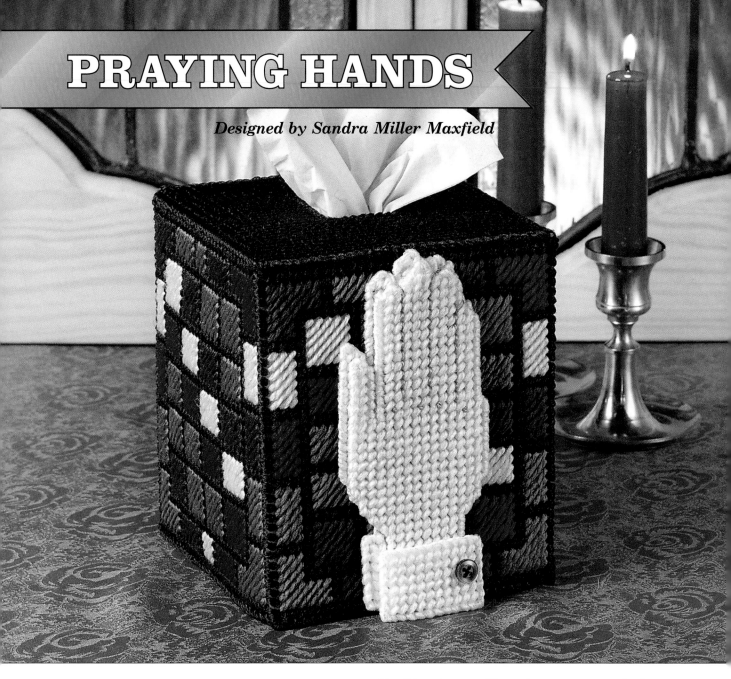

PRAYING HANDS

Designed by Sandra Miller Maxfield

SIZE: Loosely covers a boutique-style tissue box.

MATERIALS: 2½ sheets of 7-count plastic canvas; One black ¼" [6mm] round button; Sewing needle and matching color thread (optional); Craft glue or glue gun; Worsted-weight or plastic canvas yarn (for amounts see Color Key).

CUTTING INSTRUCTIONS:

A: For sides, cut four 32 x 37 holes.
B: For top, cut one according to graph.
C: For hands, cut two according to graph.

D: For top cuff, cut one 7 x 11 holes.
E: For bottom cuff, cut one 2 x 7 holes (no graph).
F: For optional bottom and flap, cut one 32 x 32 holes for bottom and one 12 x 32 holes for flap (no graph).

STITCHING INSTRUCTIONS:

NOTE: F pieces are not worked.

1: Using colors and stitches indicated, work A, B, one C for front and D pieces according to graphs; work remaining C above placement lines only. Using white and Continental Stitch, work E. With matching colors, Overcast cutout edges of B and edges of C-E pieces.

2: Using six strands floss and embroidery stitches indicated, embroider detail on front C piece as indicated on graph.

3: With black, Whipstitch A and B pieces together to form Cover; Whipstitch F pieces together and to Cover side. Overcast unfinished edges.

4: Glue or sew button to top cuff as indicated. Glue top cuff to front hand and bottom cuff to remaining hand; glue hands together as indicated.

5: Glue hand assembly to one side of Tissue Cover as shown in photo.✢

B – Top (cut 1) 32 x 32 hole

Cut Out

D – Top Cuff
(cut 1)
7 x 11 holes

A – Side (cut 4) 32 x 37 holes

C – Hand
(cut 2) 15 x 36 holes

COLOR KEY: Praying Hands

Embroidery floss			AMOUNT
▪ Toast			3 yds. [2.7m]

Worsted-weight	Nylon Plus™	Need-loft®	YARN AMOUNT
■ Black	#02	#00	60 yds. [54.9m]
▫ Flesh Tone	–	#56	12 yds. [11m]
▫ Holly	#31	#27	12 yds. [11m]
▫ Purple	#21	#46	12 yds. [11m]
▫ Red	#20	#01	12 yds. [11m]
▫ Royal	#09	#32	12 yds. [11m]
▫ Yellow	#26	#57	12 yds. [11m]
▫ White	#01	#41	2 yds. [1.8m]

STITCH KEY:

— Backstitch/Straight
● French Knot
◆ Button Attachment
— Top Cuff Placement
— Bottom Cuff Placement
— Hand Placement

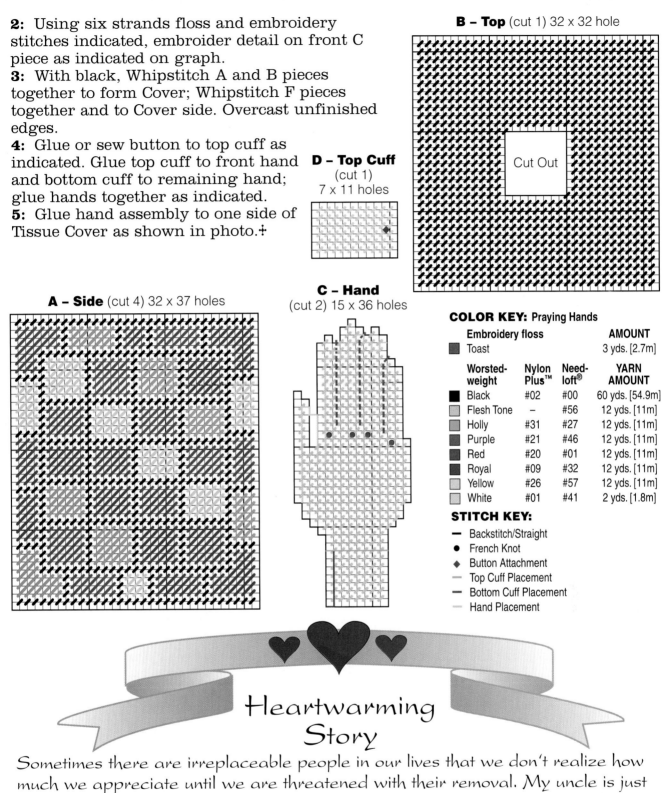

Heartwarming Story

Sometimes there are irreplaceable people in our lives that we don't realize how much we appreciate until we are threatened with their removal. My uncle is just such a person. He has always prayed for everyone he comes across. He keeps a prayer list and adds to it, but never takes away from it. Every morning, he gets up at 5:30 to begin his prayers. He sends these people a card every year with a scripture and his phone number in case they ever want to call him. No one really focused on the gift he gave until two years ago. We found out he was dying of brain cancer. He never once asked anyone to pray for him, but everyone did. It was his only line of defense. When we heard that his cancer was receding, we realized just how powerful prayer can be. – Kim Votaw

LIL' SCHOLAR'S WREATH

Designed by Robin Petrina

Gift Idea

Reward your favorite educator by putting the wreath on top of a gift box filled with crafting materials for her class, or fill it with pampering goodies, such as bath salts, lotion, a buck wheat eye pillow or aroma therapy oils.

SIZE: Wreath is about 10½" x 11¾" [26.7cm x 29.8cm].

MATERIALS: 1½ sheets of 7-count plastic canvas; One 9½" [24.1cm] plastic canvas radial circle; One 9" x 12" [22.9cm x 30.5cm] sheet of black felt; Craft glue or glue gun; Metallic cord (for amount see Color Key); Worsted-weight or plastic canvas yarn (for amounts see Color Key).

CUTTING INSTRUCTIONS:

NOTE: Graphs continued on page 124.

A: For base, cut away one outer row and twenty inner rows of holes from circle, leaving a 9"-across [22.9cm] ring of eight rows (no graph).

B: For schoolhouse, cut one according to graph.

C: For ruler, cut one 8 x 39 holes.

D: For book, cut one 13 x 17 holes.

E: For pencils, cut two according to graph.

F: For crayons, cut two according to graph.

G: For letter "A," cut one according to graph.

H: For letter "B," cut one according to graph.

I: For letter "C," cut one according to graph.

J: For number "1," cut one according to graph.

K: For number "2," cut one according to graph.

L: For number "3," cut one according to graph.

M: For apples, cut two according to graph.

N: For leaves, cut two according to graph.

STITCHING INSTRUCTIONS:

NOTE: A piece is not worked.

1: Using colors and stitches indicated, work B-E, one F and G-N pieces according to graphs; substituting sail blue for lilac and royal for purple, work remaining F piece according to graph.

2: With camel for schoolhouse bell (see photo) and apple stems, red for schoolhouse tower, black for pencil points and with matching colors, Overcast edges of B-N pieces.

3: Using colors (Separate into individual plies, if desired.) and embroidery stitches indicated, embroider detail on B-F pieces as indicated on graphs.

NOTE: For wreath lining, using A piece as a pattern, cut one from felt ⅛" [3mm] smaller at all edges.

4: Glue felt to A piece; glue leaves to apples and B-M pieces to felt as desired or as shown. Hang as desired.✢

C – Ruler
(cut 1) 8 x 39 holes

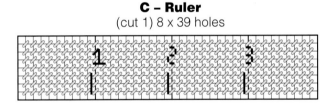

COLOR KEY: Lil' Scholar's Wreath

Metallic cord			AMOUNT
Silver/White			1 yd. [0.9m]

Worsted-weight	Nylon Plus™	Needloft®	YARN AMOUNT
Yellow	#26	#57	16 yds. [14.6m]
Xmas Red	#19	#02	14 yds. [12.8m]
Lilac	#22	#45	9 yds. [8.2m]
Bright Orange	#17	#58	6 yds. [5.5m]
Sail Blue	#04	#35	5 yds. [4.6m]
Black	#02	#00	4 yds. [3.7m]
Xmas Green	#58	#28	3 yds. [2.7m]
Camel	#34	#43	2 yds. [1.8m]
Purple	#21	#46	2 yds. [1.8m]
Holly	#31	#27	1 yd. [0.9m]
Pink	#11	#07	1 yd. [0.9m]
Royal	#09	#32	1 yd. [0.9m]
White	#01	#41	½ yd. [0.5m]

STITCH KEY:
- — Backstitch/Straight
- • French Knot

B – Schoolhouse
(cut 1)
17 x 25 holes

Cut out gray area carefully.

D – Book
(cut 1)
13 x 17 holes

E – Pencil
(cut 2)
5 x 26 holes

F – Crayon
(cut 2)
5 x 26 holes

Simple Pleasures For Special People

LIL' SCHOLAR'S WREATH

(Instructions & photo on pages 122 & 123.)

COLOR KEY: Lil' Scholar's Wreath

Metallic cord			AMOUNT
Silver/White			1 yd. [0.9m]

Worsted-weight	Nylon Plus™	Need-loft®	YARN AMOUNT
Yellow	#26	#57	16 yds. [14.6m]
Xmas Red	#19	#02	14 yds. [12.8m]
Lilac	#22	#45	9 yds. [8.2m]
Bright Orange	#17	#58	6 yds. [5.5m]
Sail Blue	#04	#35	5 yds. [4.6m]
Black	#02	#00	4 yds. [3.7m]
Xmas Green	#58	#28	3 yds. [2.7m]
Camel	#34	#43	2 yds. [1.8m]
Purple	#21	#46	2 yds. [1.8m]
Holly	#31	#27	1 yd. [0.9m]
Pink	#11	#07	1 yd. [0.9m]
Royal	#09	#32	1 yd. [0.9m]
White	#01	#41	½ yd. [0.5m]

STITCH KEY:
- — Backstitch/Straight
- • French Knot

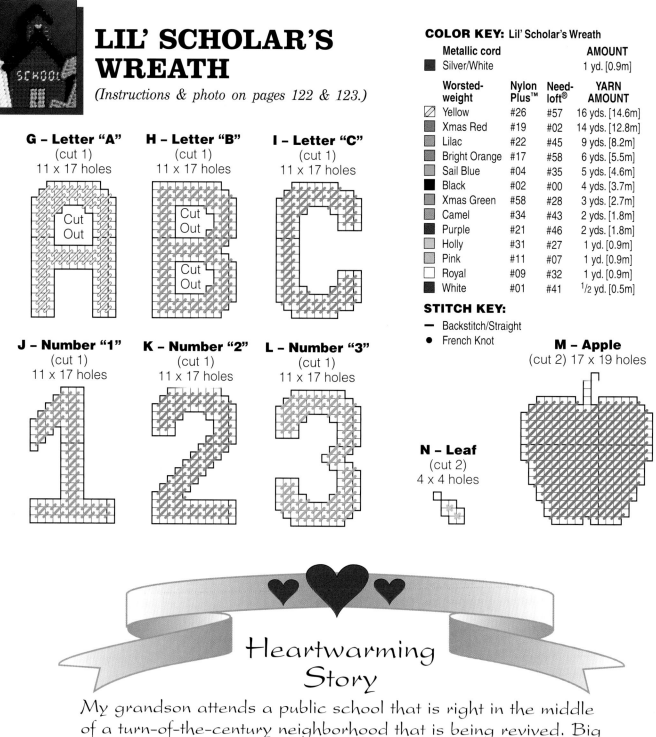

G – Letter "A" (cut 1) 11 x 17 holes

H – Letter "B" (cut 1) 11 x 17 holes

I – Letter "C" (cut 1) 11 x 17 holes

J – Number "1" (cut 1) 11 x 17 holes

K – Number "2" (cut 1) 11 x 17 holes

L – Number "3" (cut 1) 11 x 17 holes

M – Apple (cut 2) 17 x 19 holes

N – Leaf (cut 2) 4 x 4 holes

Heartwarming Story

My grandson attends a public school that is right in the middle of a turn-of-the-century neighborhood that is being revived. Big Victorian mansions are being refurbished by the wealthy, while small, fixer-upper bungalows are being made over for the newly-graduated professional. But, close by are the rather run-down sections that are what we might classify as "inner-city poverty." The teachers have gracefully intergrated the children into a harmonious learning environment where there is peace and tranquility. One reason for this school's success is that their focus is on encouraging creativity. The philosophy is, once one experiences the joys of creativity, destructive tendencies lessen. - Donna Robertson

BEJEWELED BASKETS

Designed by Sandra Miller Maxfield

Instructions on next page

BEJEWELED BASKETS

(Photo on page 125.)

SIZES: Basket #1 is 5⅞" x 6⅜" x 3¼" tall [15cm x 16.2cm x 8.2cm]; Basket #2 is 3½" square x 3¼" tall [8.9cm x 8.2cm]; Basket #3 is 3¾" across x 3¼" tall [9.5cm x 8.2cm]. Sizes do not including handles.

MATERIALS: Two sheets of black 7-count plastic canvas; Fifty-six assorted-color 10mm stones; Forty assorted-color 5mm stones; Sixteen gold 5mm half-beads; Craft glue or glue gun; Worsted-weight or plastic canvas yarn (for amount see Color Key).

CUTTING INSTRUCTIONS:
A: For side pieces, cut ten according to graph.
B: For round side, cut one according to graph.
C: For bottom #1, cut one according to graph.
D: For bottom #2, cut one 14 x 14 holes.
E: For bottom #3, cut one according to graph.
F: For handles, cut three 3 x 65 holes (no graph).

STITCHING INSTRUCTIONS:
NOTE: C-F pieces are not worked.
1: For Basket #1, with black, Whipstitch six A pieces together as indicated on graph and according to Basket #1 Assembly Illustration; Backstitch around lower edge according to graph, working over seams. Backstitch around upper edge as for lower edge, joining ends of one F piece on opposite sides by working through both thicknesses as one piece; Whipstitch legs of side assembly to C piece as indicated (see Illustration), Overcasting unfinished edges of C as you work.
2: For Basket #2, Whipstitch remaining A pieces together as indicated and ac-
cording to Basket #2 Assembly Illustration; Backstitch around lower edge according to graph, working over seams. Backstitch around upper edge as for lower edge, joining ends of one F piece on opposite sides by working through both thicknesses as one piece; Whipstitch legs of side assembly to D piece as indicated (see Illustration), Overcasting unfinished edges of D as you work.
3: For Basket #3, overlapping ends as indicated, using black and Backstitch, work around lower edge according to graph, working through both thicknesses at overlap area to join; Backstitch around upper edge as for lower edge, joining one end of remaining F piece at overlap (see Basket #3 Assembly Illustration) and on opposite side by working through all thicknesses as one piece. Whipstitch legs of side to E piece as indicated, Overcasting unfinished edges of E as you work.
4: Substituting gold half-beads for 5mm stones at top of Basket #2 side, glue stones to outside and inside (omit inside stones at handle attachment areas) of Baskets as indicated (see photo).✦

Tip

For an extra-fun and special way to create these bejeweled wonders, girls can arrange a slumber/work party to make them. The creators can then use them to hold lipsitcks and make-up, fun hair accessories and brushes.

B – Round Side
(cut 1) 21 x 75 holes
Cut out gray areas carefully.

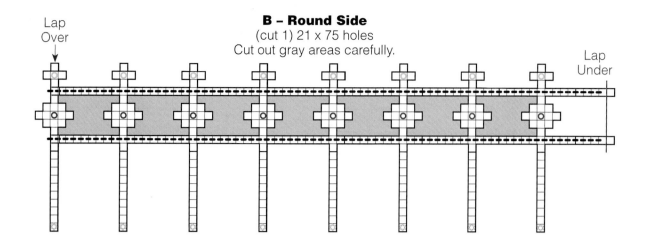

Lap Over

Lap Under

A – Side Piece
(cut 10) 20 x 21 holes
Cut out gray areas carefully.

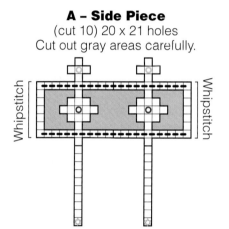

Whipstitch

Whipstitch

C – Bottom #1
(cut 1)
23 x 23 holes

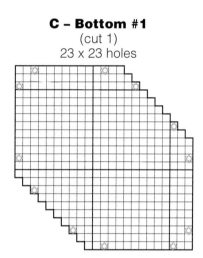

D – Bottom #2
(cut 1)
14 x 14 holes

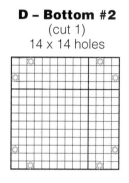

COLOR KEY: Bejeweled Baskets

Worsted-weight	Nylon Plus™	Need-loft®	YARN AMOUNT
■ Black	#02	#00	22 yds. [20.1m]

PLACEMENT KEY:
✿ Side Attachment
⊙ 10mm Stone
○ 5mm Stone

E – Bottom #3
(cut 1)
15 x 15 holes

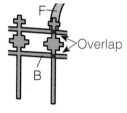

Basket #3 Assembly Illustration

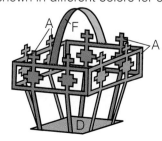

F

Overlap

B

Basket #1 Assembly Illustration
(Pieces are shown in different colors for contrast.)

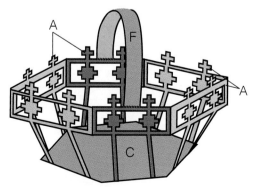

A

F

A

C

Basket #2 Assembly Illustration
(Pieces shown in different colors for contrast.)

A

F

A

D

Gift Idea

Stitch this cute and useful School Bus as a special gift for all those wonderful people who help your little one make the passage into the world every school day. It makes a great gift for the school bus driver or crossing guard when filled with small amenities like chap stick, hand warmers or a muffler.

SIZE: $3\frac{7}{8}$" x $6\frac{1}{4}$" x $3\frac{7}{8}$" [9.8cm x 15.9cm x 9.8cm], not including handles.

MATERIALS: $1\frac{1}{2}$ sheets of 7-count plastic canvas; Four yellow $\frac{1}{2}$" [13mm] buttons; #3 pearl cotton or six-strand embroidery floss (for amounts see Color Key); Worsted-weight or plastic canvas yarn (for amounts see Color Key).

CUTTING INSTRUCTIONS:

A: For sides, cut two 25 x 41 holes.
B: For ends, cut two 25 x 25 holes.
C: For bottom, cut one 25 x 41 holes.
D: For handles, cut two 5 x 73 holes.

STITCHING INSTRUCTIONS:

1: Using colors and stitches indicated, work A-D pieces according to graphs; with royal, Overcast edges of D pieces.
2: Using pearl cotton or six strands floss in colors and embroidery stitches indicated, embroider detail on A pieces as indicated on graph.
3: With royal, Whipstitch A-C pieces together; Overcast unfinished edges.
4: With red pearl cotton or floss, working through all thicknesses, sew buttons to handles and handles to sides as indicated on A and D graphs.✝

A – Side
(cut 2) 25 x 41 holes

B – End
(cut 2) 25 x 25 holes

D – Handle
(cut 2)
5 x 73 holes

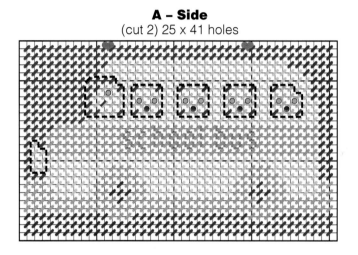

C – Bottom
(cut 1) 25 x 41 holes

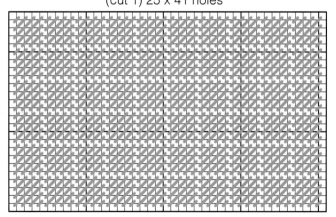

COLOR KEY: School Bus

#3 pearl cotton or floss		AMOUNT
■	Black	4 yds. [3.7m]
▨	Yellow	3 yds. [2.7m]
▨	Blue	2 yds. [1.8m]
■	Red	2 yds. [1.8m]

Worsted-weight	Nylon Plus™	Needloft®	YARN AMOUNT
■ Xmas Green	#58	#28	36 yds. [32.9m]
■ Royal	#09	#32	25 yds. [22.9m]
▢ Yellow	#26	#57	20 yds. [18.3m]
■ Xmas Red	#19	#02	20 yds. [18.3m]
■ Black	#02	#00	12 yds. [11m]
▢ White	#01	#41	10 yds. [9.1m]
■ Gray	#23	#38	8 yds. [7.3m]
▨ Coral	#14	#66	4 yds. [3.7m]

STITCH KEY:
— Backstitch/Straight
● French Knot
♥ Handle Attachment
✳ Button Attachment

BAKING CUPS

Designed by
Betty Frew

Gift Idea

Fill these versatile Baking Cups
with goodies baked in disposable
cupcake cups. They can also
be filled with candy or other tradi-
tional stocking stuffers. Give
them to special people in nursing
homes or use them as party favors
for the bowling club, garden
club or needlework club.

SIZE: Each is about 2⅞" across x 3⅜" tall [7.3cm x 8.6cm], including handle.

MATERIALS FOR ONE: ¼ sheet of white 7-count plastic canvas; One Darice® 4¼" [10.8cm] half-radial plastic canvas circle; Craft glue or glue gun; Six-strand metallic embroidery floss or medium metallic braid (for amount see Color Key); Worsted-weight or plastic canvas yarn(for amounts see Color Key).

CUTTING INSTRUCTIONS:
A: For bottom, cut one according to graph.
B: For side, cut one 8 x 58 holes.

C: For handle, cut one 3 x 45 holes.

STITCHING INSTRUCTIONS:
NOTE: Uncoded areas of B and C pieces may be left unworked or worked using white and Continental Stitch.
1: Using colors and stitches indicated, work B piece according to graph.
2: Using six strands floss or braid and embroidery stitches indicated, embroider detail on B and C pieces as indicated on graphs.
3: With white, Whipstitch ends of B piece together as indicated. Whipstitch B to A; if desired, Overcast unfinished edges.
4: Glue handle ends to inside of Basket as indicated.✛

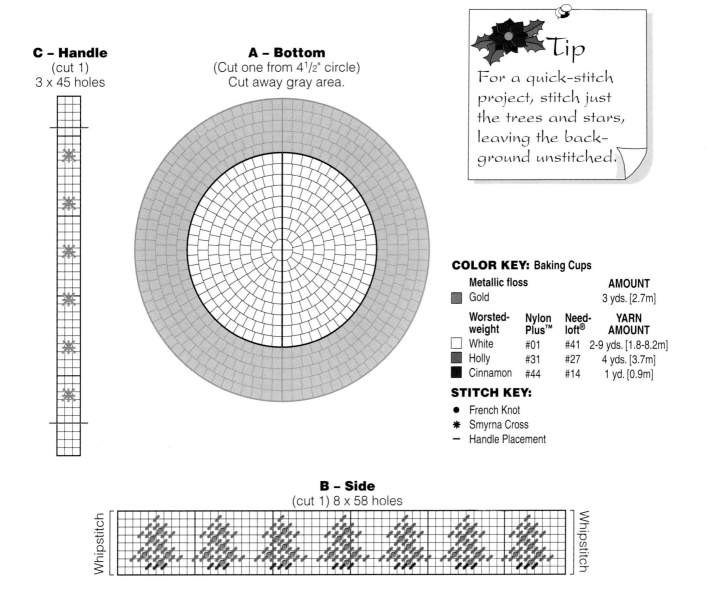

C – Handle
(cut 1)
3 x 45 holes

A – Bottom
(Cut one from 4½" circle)
Cut away gray area.

Tip
For a quick-stitch project, stitch just the trees and stars, leaving the background unstitched.

COLOR KEY: Baking Cups

Metallic floss			AMOUNT
▨ Gold			3 yds. [2.7m]

Worsted-weight	Nylon Plus™	Need-loft®	YARN AMOUNT
☐ White	#01	#41	2-9 yds. [1.8-8.2m]
▨ Holly	#31	#27	4 yds. [3.7m]
■ Cinnamon	#44	#14	1 yd. [0.9m]

STITCH KEY:
● French Knot
✳ Smyrna Cross
– Handle Placement

B – Side
(cut 1) 8 x 58 holes

Whipstitch

Whipstitch

HOLIDAY PINS

Designed by
Celia Lange Designs

SIZES: Jingle Pin is 1½" x 3" [3.8cm x 7.6cm], FaLaLa Pin is 1⅛" x 3½" [2.9cm x 8.9cm], not including charms.

MATERIALS: Scraps of 10-count plastic canvas; Two red ⅜" [10mm] jingle bells; Three brass ½"-¾" [13-19mm] music charms; Three gold jump rings; Two gold 1" [2.5cm] pinbacks; Craft glue or glue gun; ⅛" [3mm] metallic ribbon or heavy metallic braid (for amount see Color Key); #3 pearl cotton or six-strand embroidery floss (for amounts see Color Key).

CUTTING INSTRUCTIONS:
A: For Jingle, cut one according to graph.

B: For FaLaLa, cut one according to graph.

STITCHING INSTRUCTIONS:
1: Using pearl cotton or six strands floss in colors and stitches indicated, work A and B pieces according to graphs; with ribbon or braid, Overcast edges.
2: With ribbon, tack jingle bells to wrong side of A as indicated on graph; using jump rings, attach music charms to B as indicated.
3: Glue one pinback to wrong side of each piece.✝

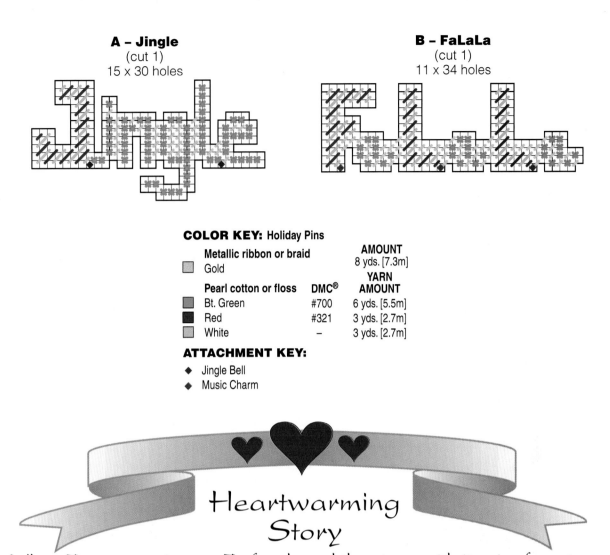

A – Jingle
(cut 1)
15 x 30 holes

B – FaLaLa
(cut 1)
11 x 34 holes

COLOR KEY: Holiday Pins

	Metallic ribbon or braid		AMOUNT
	Gold		8 yds. [7.3m]

	Pearl cotton or floss	DMC®	YARN AMOUNT
	Bt. Green	#700	6 yds. [5.5m]
	Red	#321	3 yds. [2.7m]
	White	–	3 yds. [2.7m]

ATTACHMENT KEY:
◆ Jingle Bell
◆ Music Charm

Heartwarming Story

When I was growing up I often heard the story, with its air of mystery and intrigue, of Aunt Mary's disappearance. You see, Aunt Mary worked in the big city and only took the bus home every other weekend. One weekend in 1948, she didn't come home. Through the years, much time and effort went into searching for Aunt Mary. Although the clues seemed to say she was still living, following them only lead down blind alleys. Another aunt of mine never gave up the search and after forty-five years, discovered Aunt Mary's whereabouts.

Much fuss was made and many family members went to visit her, gathering pieces and parts to her secret life to share with the rest of us - Aunt Mary had married a dashing young man from the circus and had run away with him to become a travelling performer. At our next big holiday get-together, Aunt Mary flew to our home state and joined us for a family reunion. With her, she brought 50 hand-stitched, plastic canvas Christmas wreath lapel pins as a token gift for each family member. Somehow the little wreath humanized the whole scene and we enjoyed laughing and chatting about how we had a common love of stitching. You don't have to do anything as dramatic as Aunt Mary to stitch these lapel pins for your loved ones, they'll be appreciated even if you never run away from home! - Donna Robertson

MINI FOLK STOCKINGS

Designed by Nancy Marshall

SIZES: Each is about 5⅛" x 5¾" [13cm x 14.6cm].

MATERIALS: One 13½" x 22½" [34.3cm x 57.2cm] sheet of 7-count plastic canvas; Worsted-weight or plastic canvas yarn (for amounts see Color Key).

CUTTING INSTRUCTIONS:

A: For Stocking #1, cut two according to graph.

B: For Stocking #2, cut two according to graph.

C: For Stocking #3, cut two according to graph.

STITCHING INSTRUCTIONS:

1: Using colors and stitches indicated, work A-C pieces (one each on opposite side of canvas) according to graphs.

2: Holding corresponding pieces wrong sides together, with Xmas green for A, Xmas red for B and bt. orange for C, Whipstitch each Stocking together as indicated on graphs.

3: With Xmas red for Stocking #1, Xmas green for Stocking #2 and with white for Stocking #3, Overcast unfinished edges.

NOTE: Cut one 5" [12.7cm] length each of Xmas red, Xmas green and bt. orange.

4: For each hanger, with matching Whipstitch color, thread one strand of yarn through all thicknesses at ✦ hole as indicated; bring ends to even and tie into a knot.✣

Tip

Quickly make a dozen of these gift stockings by stitching only the top rows of the design on colored plastic canvas.

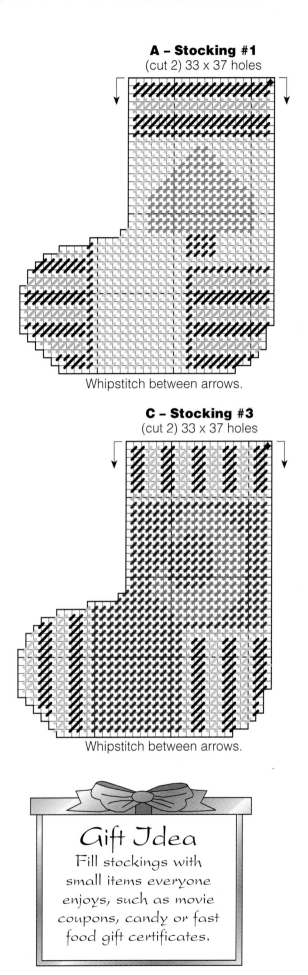

A – Stocking #1
(cut 2) 33 x 37 holes

Whipstitch between arrows.

B – Stocking #2
(cut 2) 33 x 37 holes

Whipstitch between arrows.

C – Stocking #3
(cut 2) 33 x 37 holes

Whipstitch between arrows.

COLOR KEY: Mini Folk Stockings

	Worsted-weight	Nylon Plus™	Need-loft®	YARN AMOUNT
	Yellow	#26	#57	22 yds. [20.1m]
	White	#01	#41	21 yds. [19.2m]
	Black	#02	#00	20 yds. [18.3m]
	Xmas Red	#19	#02	12 yds. [11m]
	Royal	#09	#32	10 yds. [9.1m]
	Xmas Green	#58	#28	10 yds. [9.1m]
	Bt. Orange	#17	#58	8 yds. [7.3m]

ATTACHMENT:
✦ Hanger Attachment

Gift Idea
Fill stockings with small items everyone enjoys, such as movie coupons, candy or fast food gift certificates.

Growing Traditions for the Gardener

Chapter Seven

Gift Idea

Create a basket of
goodies for your bird-watching
friends. Fill it with packages
of bird seed and an encyclo-
pedia of birds, along with this
wintery welcome for your
feathery friends.

SIZE: 5³⁄₈" x 11¹⁄₄" [13.7cm x 28.6cm], not including hanger.

MATERIALS: 1½ sheets of 7-count plastic canvas; 18" [45.7cm] length of green 20-gauge floral wire; 4¼" x 10" [10.8cm x 25.4cm] piece of cardboard; Pencil; Craft glue or glue gun; #3 pearl cotton or six-strand embroidery floss (for amounts see Color Key); Worsted-weight or plastic canvas yarn (for amounts see Color Key).

CUTTING INSTRUCTIONS:
A: For sign, cut one according to graph.

B: For houses #1-#4, cut one each according to graphs.
C: For roofs #1-#4, cut one each according to graphs.
D: For branches #1 and #2, cut one each according to graphs.
E: For birds #1 and #2, cut one each according to graphs.
F: For wings #1 and #2, cut one each according to graphs.

STITCHING INSTRUCTIONS:
1: Using colors and stitches indicated, work pieces according to graphs; fill in uncoded area of A using sail blue and

Continental Stitch.

2: With denim for top and sandstone for bottom of sign as shown in photo, Overcast edges of A; with watermelon for house #1, teal blue for house #4 and with matching colors as shown, Overcast edges of remaining pieces.

3: Using pearl cotton or six strands floss in colors and embroidery stitches indicated, embroider letters on A and eyes on E pieces as indicated on graphs.

4: Using yarn in colors indicated and Backstitch, embroider border detail on A, B#2 and B#3 pieces as indicated.

5: Loosely curl wire around a pencil and stretch to lengthen. For hanger, insert one end of wire from front to back at each ▲ hole on A as indicated; bend wire ends up on wrong side to secure.

6: Glue B-F pieces together and to A as desired or as shown.✢

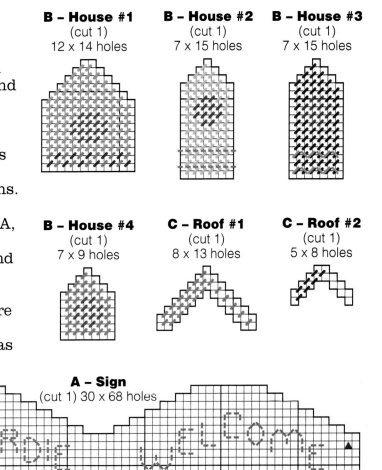

B – House #1
(cut 1)
12 x 14 holes

B – House #2
(cut 1)
7 x 15 holes

B – House #3
(cut 1)
7 x 15 holes

B – House #4
(cut 1)
7 x 9 holes

C – Roof #1
(cut 1)
8 x 13 holes

C – Roof #2
(cut 1)
5 x 8 holes

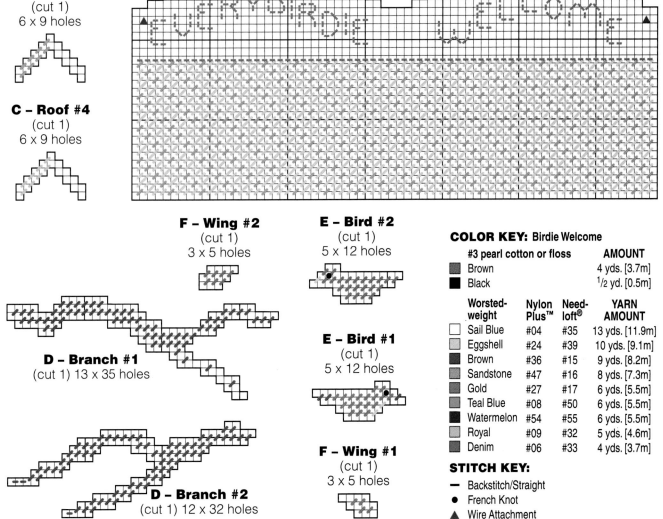

C – Roof #3
(cut 1)
6 x 9 holes

C – Roof #4
(cut 1)
6 x 9 holes

A – Sign
(cut 1) 30 x 68 holes

F – Wing #2
(cut 1)
3 x 5 holes

E – Bird #2
(cut 1)
5 x 12 holes

D – Branch #1
(cut 1) 13 x 35 holes

E – Bird #1
(cut 1)
5 x 12 holes

D – Branch #2
(cut 1) 12 x 32 holes

F – Wing #1
(cut 1)
3 x 5 holes

COLOR KEY: Birdie Welcome

#3 pearl cotton or floss			AMOUNT
▨ Brown			4 yds. [3.7m]
■ Black			1/2 yd. [0.5m]

Worsted-weight	Nylon Plus™	Need-loft®	YARN AMOUNT
□ Sail Blue	#04	#35	13 yds. [11.9m]
▨ Eggshell	#24	#39	10 yds. [9.1m]
▨ Brown	#36	#15	9 yds. [8.2m]
▨ Sandstone	#47	#16	8 yds. [7.3m]
▨ Gold	#27	#17	6 yds. [5.5m]
▨ Teal Blue	#08	#50	6 yds. [5.5m]
▨ Watermelon	#54	#55	6 yds. [5.5m]
▨ Royal	#09	#32	5 yds. [4.6m]
▨ Denim	#06	#33	4 yds. [3.7m]

STITCH KEY:
— Backstitch/Straight
● French Knot
▲ Wire Attachment

BUMBLE BEE BOOKEND

Designed by Michele Wilcox

Gift Idea

Include a book store gift certificate with the present of Bumble Bee Bookend.

SIZE: 2¼" x 5" x 5¾" [5.7cm x 12.7cm x 14.6cm]; covers a standard 5" [12.7cm] metal bookend.

MATERIALS: One sheet of 7-count plastic canvas; #3 pearl cotton or six-strand embroidery floss (for amount see Color Key); Worsted-weight or plastic canvas yarn (for amounts see Color Key).

CUTTING INSTRUCTIONS:

A: For front and backing, cut two (one for front and one for backing) 32 x 36 holes.
B: For base and backing, cut two (one for base and one for backing) 13 x 32 holes.

STITCHING INSTRUCTIONS:

NOTE: Backing pieces are not worked.
1: Using colors indicated and Continental Stitch, work one A piece for front and one B piece for base according to graphs; fill in uncoded areas using royal and Continental Stitch.
2: Using black (Separate into individual plies, if desired.) and pearl cotton or six strands floss and embroidery stitches indicated, embroider detail on front A as indicated on graph.
3: With royal, Whipstitch pieces together as indicated and according to Bookend Assembly Diagram.✝

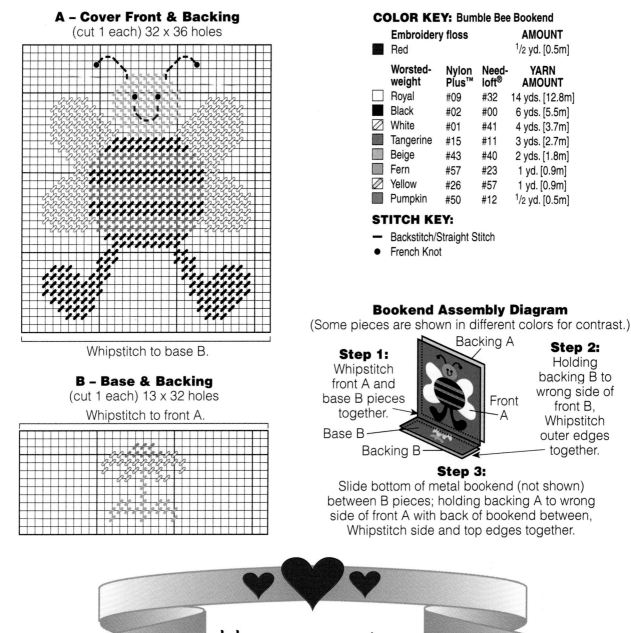

A – Cover Front & Backing
(cut 1 each) 32 x 36 holes

Whipstitch to base B.

B – Base & Backing
(cut 1 each) 13 x 32 holes

Whipstitch to front A.

COLOR KEY: Bumble Bee Bookend

Embroidery floss			AMOUNT
■ Red			1/2 yd. [0.5m]

Worsted-weight	Nylon Plus™	Need-loft®	YARN AMOUNT
☐ Royal	#09	#32	14 yds. [12.8m]
■ Black	#02	#00	6 yds. [5.5m]
▨ White	#01	#41	4 yds. [3.7m]
▨ Tangerine	#15	#11	3 yds. [2.7m]
▨ Beige	#43	#40	2 yds. [1.8m]
▨ Fern	#57	#23	1 yd. [0.9m]
▨ Yellow	#26	#57	1 yd. [0.9m]
▨ Pumpkin	#50	#12	1/2 yd. [0.5m]

STITCH KEY:

– Backstitch/Straight Stitch
● French Knot

Bookend Assembly Diagram
(Some pieces are shown in different colors for contrast.)

Step 1:
Whipstitch front A and base B pieces together.

Backing A
Base B
Backing B
Front A

Step 2:
Holding backing B to wrong side of front B, Whipstitch outer edges together.

Step 3:
Slide bottom of metal bookend (not shown) between B pieces; holding backing A to wrong side of front A with back of bookend between, Whipstitch side and top edges together.

Heartwarming Story

I love growing herbs. My favorite is Basil, and all my friends have grown accustomed to seeing my two big pots of Basil by the front porch of my home. It's the best spot for the morning sun and afternoon shade that Basil loves so much. And bags of frozen, crushed basil lie safely in my freezer, waiting for the winter pots of homemade soup that I love to make. If I can't spend my time outdoors tending to the herbs I love so much, then let me be inside reading about them or cooking with them! One of my more memorable Christmas presents was a generous gift certificate to a local bookstore that catered to a gardening and cooking enthusiast. I was able to buy several books on herb gardening and cooking with herbs, while there were still weeks of less-than-desirable weather for gardening ahead of me. I found planning my garden was a pleasant way to spend a yucky winter's evening. – Donna Robertson

CRAFT BASKET

Designed by Dawn Austin

SIZE: 6⅝" x 9" x 5½" tall [16.8cm x 22.9cm x 14cm], not including handle.

MATERIALS: Four sheets of 7-count plastic canvas; Velcro® closure (optional); Craft glue or glue gun; Worsted-weight or plastic canvas yarn (for amounts see Color Key).

CUTTING INSTRUCTIONS:

NOTE: Graphs continued on page 144.

A: For box sides, cut two according to graph.

B: For box ends, cut two according to graph.

C: For box bottom pieces, cut two 39 x 55 holes (no graph).

D: For lip support, cut one according to graph.

E: For lip sides, cut two according to graph.

F: For lip ends, cut two according to graph.

G: For handle, cut one according to graph.

H: For handle tabs, cut two 3 x 8 holes.

I: For lid top, cut one 35 x 51 holes.

J: For lid sides, cut two according to graph.

K: For lid ends, cut two according to graph.

L: For latch, cut one according to graph.

M: For flower blossoms, cut eleven according to graph.
N: For flower stems, cut eleven according to graph.

STITCHING INSTRUCTIONS:
NOTE: C pieces are not worked.
1: Using colors and stitches indicated, work A, B and D-N pieces according to graphs; with navy, Overcast edges of G. With white, Overcast long edges of H pieces; with matching colors, Overcast edges of M and N pieces.
2: Whipstitch and assemble A-L pieces as indicated on graphs and according to Basket Assembly Diagram on page 144.
3: Glue flower stems and blossoms to Basket as desired or as shown in photo.✢

COLOR KEY: Craft Basket

Worsted-weight	Nylon Plus™	Need-loft®	YARN AMOUNT
■ Navy	#45	#31	50 yds. [45.7m]
▨ White	#01	#41	42 yds. [38.4m]
▢ Yellow	#26	#57	13 yds. [11.9m]
▨ Holly	#31	#27	12 yds. [11m]
▨ Cinnamon	#44	#14	4 yds. [3.7m]

STITCH KEY:
▢ Handle Tab Attachment

B – Box End (cut 2) 25 x 43 holes

I – Lid Top (cut 1) 35 x 51 holes

Latch Attachment

A – Box Side (cut 2) 25 x 59 holes

M – Flower Blossom
(cut 11)
9 x 9 holes

N – Flower Stem
(cut 11)
9 x 16 holes

G – Handle
(cut 1) 10 x 74 holes

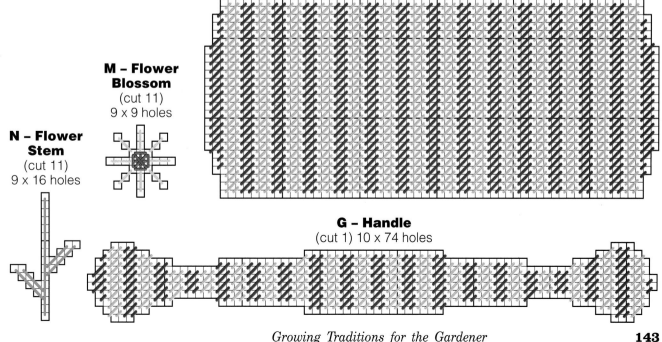

Growing Traditions for the Gardener

CRAFT BASKET

(Instructions & photo on page 142.)

E – Lip Side (cut 2) 4 x 53 holes

J – Lid Side (cut 2) 9 x 55 holes

L – Latch
(cut 1)
11 x 18 holes
Whipstitch to lid.

H – Handle Tab
(cut 2) 3 x 8 holes
Whipstitch
to I.

Whipstitch
to I.

D – Lip Support
(cut 1) 39 x 55 holes

F – Lip End (cut 2) 4 x 37 holes

K – Lid End (cut 2) 9 x 39 holes

Cut Out

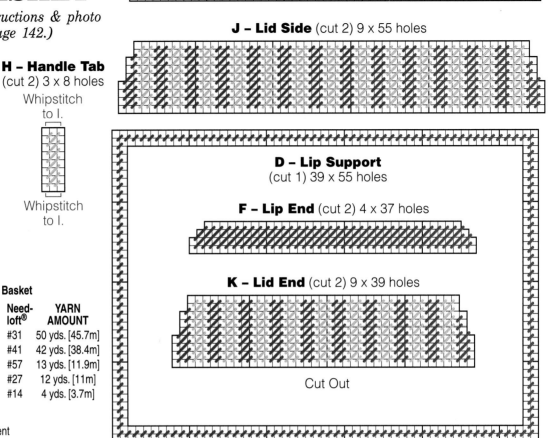

COLOR KEY: Craft Basket

	Worsted-weight	Nylon Plus™	Need-loft®	YARN AMOUNT
■	Navy	#45	#31	50 yds. [45.7m]
▨	White	#01	#41	42 yds. [38.4m]
▨	Yellow	#26	#57	13 yds. [11.9m]
▨	Holly	#31	#27	12 yds. [11m]
▨	Cinnamon	#44	#14	4 yds. [3.7m]

STITCH KEY:
☐ Handle Tab Attachment

Basket Assembly Diagram

(Pieces are shown in different colors for contrast; gray denotes wrong side.)

Step 1:
Holding G over I, with white, Whipstitch one H piece to I over each narrow end of G.

Step 2:
With navy, Whipstitch I-L pieces together; omitting lid side opposite latch attachment, Overcast unfinished edges.

Step 3:
Whipstitch A-C pieces together through all thicknesses, forming box.

Step 4:
Attaching lip pieces to inner edges on right side of lip support, Whipstitch D-F pieces together; Overcast edges of E and F pieces.

Step 5:
Leaving one side edge unjoined, Whipstitch lip support to top edges of box.

Step 6:
Whipstitch unjoined box side/lip support edge and unfinished lid side edge together through all thicknesses.

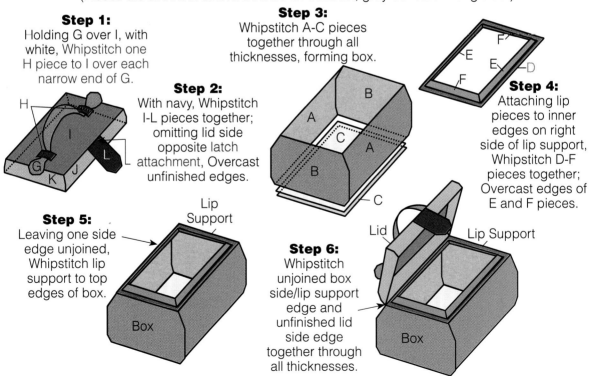

GARDEN ANGEL

*Designed by Janelle Giese
of Janelle Marie Designs*

Instructions on next page

Gift Idea

Give a gift of a Gardening Angel to someone you love with this little bit of folklore clipped with gloves and a gift certificate for gardening supplies.

GARDEN ANGEL

(Photo on page 145.)

SIZE: 6⅝" x 9¼" [16.8cm x 23.5cm].

MATERIALS: ¾ sheet of 7-count plastic canvas; 6"-wide [15.2cm] plastic chip clip; 18" [45.7cm] length of green 20-gauge floral wire; Blonde curly wool doll hair; Four small artificial pastel posies on stem wires; ½ yd. [0.5m] of lt. blue ⅛" [3mm] satin ribbon; 13 midnight rainbow 5mm glass pebble beads; Pencil; Craft glue or glue gun; #3 pearl cotton or six-strand embroidery floss (for amounts see Color Key; double amounts for floss); #5 pearl cotton or six- strand embroidery floss (for amount see Color Key); Worsted-weight or plastic canvas yarn (for amounts see Color Key).

CUTTING INSTRUCTIONS:

A: For angel, cut one according to graph.
B: For birdhouse pieces, cut two according to graph.
C: For watering can, cut one according to graph.
D: For seed pack, cut one 4 x 6 holes.
E: For trowel, cut one according to graph.

STITCHING INSTRUCTIONS:

1: Using colors indicated and Continental Stitch, work A and C-E pieces according to graphs; using a double strand of black #3 pearl cotton or 24 strands floss and Long Stitch, work center stitches on A according to graph.
2: With pink #3 pearl cotton or 12 strands floss, Overcast cutout edges of A and handle edges of E as indicated on graph. With white for seed pack, pewter for watering can and trowel and with matching colors for angel, Overcast edges of A, C and D pieces and remaining edges of E.
3: Holding B pieces together over A as indicated, using moss and Continental

Stitch, work birdhouse through all thicknesses as one piece according to B graph; omitting roof edges, Whipstitch edges of B pieces to A through all thicknesses.
4: Using black #3 pearl cotton or 12 strands floss and Straight Stitch, embroider each roof square through all thicknesses as indicated on B graph; sew beads to roof as indicated.
5: Using #3 pearl cotton or 12 strands floss in colors and embroidery stitches indicated, work cheeks, flowers and leaves on A, C and D pieces as indicated. Using #5 pearl cotton or six strands floss and embroidery stitches indicated, embroider remaining detail (work eye and mouth stitches on angel three times) on pieces as indicated.
NOTE: Cut one 7" [17.8cm] length of doll hair; cut one 6" [15.2cm] length of pink yarn.
6: For hair center part, tie hair together at center with pink strand; trim yarn close to knot. Pull a small amount of hair from each side of part and trim short for bangs. Holding part at center top of angel's head, glue hair to upper edges of head and around face (see photo).
NOTE: Cut ribbon in half.
7: For each ponytail, thread ends of one ribbon from back to front through one pair of adjacent ◆ holes on A as indicated; pull ends to even, and tie into a bow

B – Birdhouse Piece
(cut 2)
13 x 13 holes

Cut out gray area carefully.

C – Watering Can
(cut 1)
9 x 13 holes

Cut out gray area carefully.

E – Trowel
(cut 1)
5 x 7 holes
☐ Handle

D – Seed Pack
(cut 1)
4 x 6 holes

over hair tail to hold.

8: For hair garland, twist posy stems together; shape and glue garland to head over hair.

9: Loosely curl wire around a pencil and stretch to lengthen. Insert one end of wire from front to back through each ▲ hole on angel as indicated; bend wire ends

down on wrong side to secure.

10: Glue C-E pieces to apron over wire as shown in photo; glue chip clip to back above cutouts. Hang or display as desired.✝

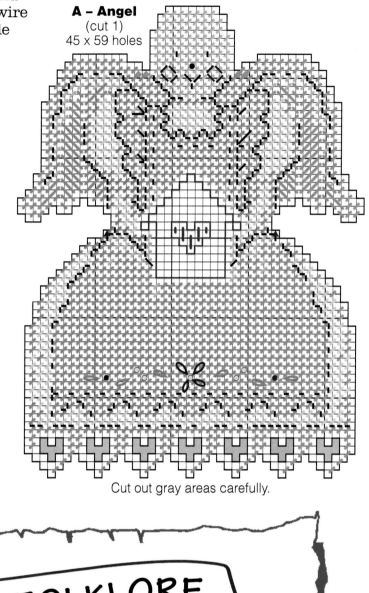

A – Angel
(cut 1)
45 x 59 holes

Cut out gray areas carefully.

COLOR KEY: Garden Angel Glove Keeper

#3 pearl cotton or floss	AMOUNT
■ Pink	5 yds. [4.6m]
■ Black	3 yds. [2.7m]
■ Mint	1 yd. [0.9m]
□ Yellow	1 yd. [0.9m]

#5 pearl cotton or floss	AMOUNT
■ Black	12 yds. [11m]

Worsted-weight	Nylon Plus™	Need-loft®	YARN AMOUNT
White	#01	#41	26 yds. [23.8m]
Peach	#46	#47	7 yds. [6.4m]
Straw	#41	#19	7 yds. [6.4m]
Baby Pink	#10	#08	3 yds. [2.7m]
Moss	#48	#25	3 yds. [2.7m]
Baby Blue	#05	#36	2 yds. [1.8m]
Pewter	#40	#65	2 yds. [1.8m]

STITCH KEY:

- — Backstitch/Straight
- ● French Knot
- ∽ Lazy Daisy
- ☐ Birdhouse Attachment
- ○ Bead Attachment
- ◆ Tie Attachment
- ▲ Wire Attachment

TALES & FOLKLORE

In old Europe, there was a tradition of having statues of angels placed all around elegant estates, especially in the gardens. Many believed that when real angels passed by and saw the statues, they would stop to greet them. This insured that the garden was a safe haven of good spirits and that the family would be blessed because of the presence of the angels.

BIRD NEST BOX

Designed by
Celia Lange Designs

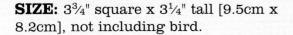

Gift Idea

Keep the fresh aroma of springtime alive in the dead of winter, by filling this lovely box with homemade potpourri. Then, give someone you love two-gifts-in-one with this darling box and aromatic potpourri for a lasting treasure.

SIZE: 3¾" square x 3¼" tall [9.5cm x 8.2cm], not including bird.

MATERIALS: One sheet of 7-count plastic canvas; 2½" [6.4cm] pink mushroom bird; Small green bird nest or green excelsior; Assorted small pink and white silk flowers and green leaves; ¼ yd. [0.2m] white fine mesh tulle; Potpourri; ½ sheet white Fun Foam; 72 white 5mm pearl beads; #9 quilting or beading needle and white quilting thread; Craft glue or glue gun;

Worsted-weight or plastic canvas yarn (for amounts see Color Key).

CUTTING INSTRUCTIONS:
A: For box sides, cut four according to graph.
B: For box bottom, cut one 21 x 21 holes (no graph).
C: For lid top, cut one 23 x 23 holes.
D: For lid sides, cut four according to graph.
E: For box side linings, using one A as

a pattern, cut four from foam ⅛" [3mm] smaller at all edges.

STITCHING INSTRUCTIONS:

1: Using colors and stitches indicated, work A, C and D pieces according to graphs; with pink, Overcast cutout edges of A pieces. Using watermelon and Continental Stitch, work B.

2: Using pink and Backstitch, embroider detail on C and D pieces as indicated on graphs.

3: With thread, sew beads to A pieces as indicated.

4: With pink, Whipstitch A and B pieces together, forming box; Whipstitch C and D pieces together, forming lid. With pink for box and white for lid, Overcast unfinished edges. Glue E pieces to inside of box.

NOTE: For potpourri bag, cut one 9"-across [22.9cm] circle of tulle.

5: Place potpourri on tulle circle; bring edges up to close. With pink yarn, tie a bow around tulle to close bag; place bag inside box.

NOTE: For excelsior nest, coil excelsior and glue into nest shape.

6: Glue nest to lid top and bird inside nest; glue silk flowers and leaves around nest as desired or as shown in photo.✛

D – Lid Side
(cut 4) 5 x 23 holes

A – Box Side
(cut 4) 19 x 21 holes

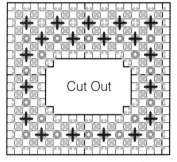

Cut Out

C – Lid Top
(cut 1) 23 x 23 holes

COLOR KEY: Bird Nest Potpourri Box

Worsted-weight	Nylon Plus™	Need-loft®	YARN AMOUNT
Pink	#11	#07	35 yds. [32m]
White	#01	#41	14 yds. [12.8m]
Watermelon	#54	#55	12 yds. [11m]

STITCH KEY:
— Backstitch/Straight
○ Bead Attachment

Tip

Make your own potpourri with fragrant flowers such as gardenias, roses, lavender or lilac. Cut the flowers (leaving a short stem), tie them with a string and hang them upside down in a cool, dry area — not in bright light. When they are completely dry, break them into pieces, or leave them whole. You can sprinkle your homemade potpourri with a purchased fragrance oil if you want to enhance the aroma.

Designed by Betty Frew

SIZES: Vase is 6" square x 5" tall [15.2cm x 12.7cm]; Plant Poke is 2¾" x 5" [7cm x 12.7cm].

MATERIALS: Two sheets of 7-count plastic canvas; Craft or ice cream stick; Craft glue or glue gun (optional); Worsted-weight or plastic canvas yarn (for amounts see Color Key).

CUTTING INSTRUCTIONS:
A: For Vase sides, cut four according to graph.
B: For Vase bottom, cut one 29 x 29 holes (no graph).
C: For Plant Poke sides, cut two according to graph.

STITCHING INSTRUCTIONS:
NOTE: B piece is not worked.
1: Using colors and stitches indicated, work A and C pieces according to graphs; with eggshell, Overcast bottom edges of C pieces as indicated on graph.
2: For Vase, with eggshell, Whipstitch A

pieces together as indicated. With fern, Whipstitch A and B pieces together; Overcast unfinished edges.

3: For Plant Poke, holding C pieces wrong sides together with stick between (Glue to secure, if desired.), with eggshell, Whipstitch unfinished edges together.✝

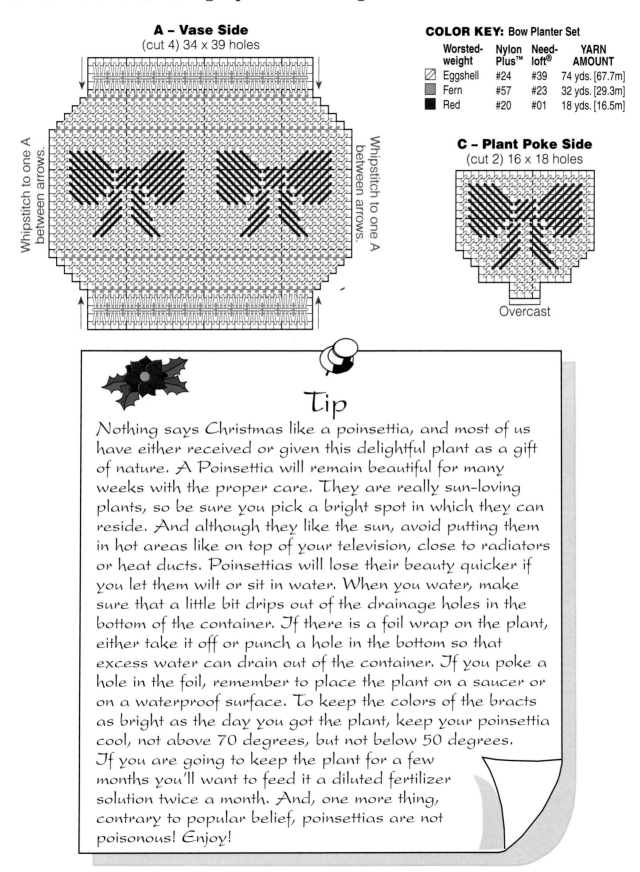

A – Vase Side
(cut 4) 34 x 39 holes

Whipstitch to one A between arrows.

Whipstitch to one A between arrows.

C – Plant Poke Side
(cut 2) 16 x 18 holes

Overcast

Tip

Nothing says Christmas like a poinsettia, and most of us have either received or given this delightful plant as a gift of nature. A Poinsettia will remain beautiful for many weeks with the proper care. They are really sun-loving plants, so be sure you pick a bright spot in which they can reside. And although they like the sun, avoid putting them in hot areas like on top of your television, close to radiators or heat ducts. Poinsettias will lose their beauty quicker if you let them wilt or sit in water. When you water, make sure that a little bit drips out of the drainage holes in the bottom of the container. If there is a foil wrap on the plant, either take it off or punch a hole in the bottom so that excess water can drain out of the container. If you poke a hole in the foil, remember to place the plant on a saucer or on a waterproof surface. To keep the colors of the bracts as bright as the day you got the plant, keep your poinsettia cool, not above 70 degrees, but not below 50 degrees. If you are going to keep the plant for a few months you'll want to feed it a diluted fertilizer solution twice a month. And, one more thing, contrary to popular belief, poinsettias are not poisonous! Enjoy!

Speed Skater Santa

Designed by Sandra Miller Maxfield

Instructions on page 155

Crescent Moon Santa

Designed by
Celia Lange Designs

Snowbirds Window

Designed by Celia Lange Designs

Instructions on
page 154

CRESCENT MOON SANTA

SIZE: 3¼" x 4¼" [8.2cm x 10.8cm].

MATERIALS: Scraps of 7-count plastic canvas; Gold 9mm jingle bell; Two miniature artificial pinecones; Three miniature 1" [2.5cm] pieces of artificial evergreen stem; Craft glue or glue gun; Medium metallic braid or metallic cord (for amounts see Color Key); #3 pearl cotton or six-strand embroidery floss (for amounts see Color Key); Worsted-weight or plastic canvas yarn (for amounts see Color Key).

CUTTING INSTRUCTIONS:

A: For head, cut one according to graph.
B: For hat cuff, cut one according to graph.
C: For mustache pieces, cut two according to graph.

STITCHING INSTRUCTIONS:

1: Using colors indicated and Continental Stitch, work A and B pieces according to graphs; with white for mustache pieces and with matching colors, Overcast edges of A-C pieces.
2: Using metallic braid or cord in colors indicated and Backstitch, embroider detail on A and B pieces as indicated on graphs; using pearl cotton or six strands floss in colors indicated and French Knot, embroider facial detail on A as indicated.
3: With red braid or cord, sew bell to tip of hat as shown in photo; glue artificial pinecones and greenery and B and C pieces to A as shown.
4: For hanger, secure ends of a 2" [5.1cm] strand of red yarn on wrong side at top of Ornament, or hang as desired.

A – Crescent Santa Head
(cut 1) 21 x 27 holes

B – Crescent Santa Hat Cuff
(cut 1) 5 x 12 holes

C – Crescent Santa Mustache Piece
(cut 2) 2 x 3 holes

COLOR KEY: Crescent Moon Santa

Med. metallic braid or cord		AMOUNT
■	Red	3 yds. [2.7m]
■	Pearl/White	2 yds. [1.8m]

Pearl cotton or floss		AMOUNT
■	Blue	¼ yd. [0.2m]
■	Pink	¼ yd. [0.2m]

Worsted-weight	Nylon Plus™	Need-loft®	YARN AMOUNT
■ White	#01	#41	6 yds. [5.5m]
■ Red	#20	#01	4 yds. [3.7m]
■ Flesh Tone	–	#56	1 yd. [0.9m]
■ Baby Pink	#10	#08	½ yd. [0.5m]

STITCH KEY:
— Backstitch/Straight
● French Knot

Tip

Turn this delightful ornament into a suncatcher by adding a crystal pendant to dangle from the crescent moon.

WINTER LANDSCAPE

(Photo on page 152.)

SNOWBIRDS WINDOW

SIZE: 2⅝" x 4⅜" [6.7cm x 11.1cm], not including birds.

MATERIALS: Scraps of 7-count plastic canvas; Two 1¼" [3.2cm] cardinal buttons; Craft glue or glue gun; #3 pearl cotton or six-strand embroidery floss (for amounts see Color Key); Worsted-weight or plastic canvas yarn (for amounts see Color Key).

CUTTING INSTRUCTIONS:

A: For picture, cut one 15 x 26 holes.
B: For frame, cut one according to graph.

STITCHING INSTRUCTIONS:

1: Using colors and stitches indicated, work pieces according to graphs; with holly, Overcast edges.
2: Using pearl cotton or six strands floss in colors indicated and Backstitch, embroider letters on A as indicated on graph.
3: Glue B to right side of A and buttons to frame as desired or as shown.
4: For hanger, secure ends of a 2" [5.1cm] strand of holly yarn on wrong side at top of Ornament, or hang as desired.

A – Snowbirds Picture
(cut 1) 15 x 26 holes

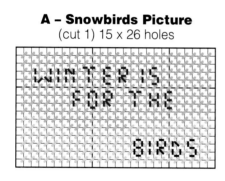

B – Snowbirds Frame
(cut 1) 17 x 28 holes

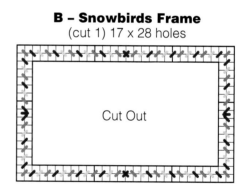

Cut Out

Tip

Make these ornaments into whimsical picture frames! All you have to do is stitch the outer rim of the ornament, cutting the blank plastic from the center. Then, cut plastic canvas for a backing, and whipstitch around three sides, leaving one open to insert a clear plastic cover with your photo in it.

COLOR KEY: Snowbirds Window

Pearl cotton or floss			AMOUNT
■ White			2 yds. [1.8m]
■ Red			1 yd. [0.9m]

Worsted-weight	Nylon Plus™	Need-loft®	YARN AMOUNT
Royal	#09	#32	7 yds. [6.4m]
White	#01	#41	6 yds. [5.5m]
Holly	#31	#27	5 yds. [4.6m]
Red	#20	#01	1 yd. [0.9m]

STITCH KEY:
— Backstitch/Straight

SPEED SKATER SANTA

SIZE: 4½" x 4¾" [11.4cm x 12.1cm].

MATERIALS: ¼ sheet of 7-count plastic canvas; Two 1¼" [3.2cm] paper clips; Craft glue or glue gun; Worsted-weight or plastic canvas yarn (for amounts see Color Key).

CUTTING INSTRUCTIONS:
For Speed Skater Santa, cut one according to graph.

STITCHING INSTRUCTIONS:
1: Using colors and stitches indicated, work piece according to graph; with matching colors, Overcast edges.
2: Using black (Separate into individual plies, if desired.) and embroidery stitches indicated, embroider detail as indicated on graph.
3: With black, tack one paper clip to each boot as indicated.
4: Hang as desired.✝

COLOR KEY: Speed Skater Santa

	Worsted-weight	Nylon Plus™	Need-loft®	YARN AMOUNT
■	Red	#20	#01	5 yds. [4.6m]
■	White	#01	#41	4 yds. [3.7m]
■	Black	#02	#00	3 yds. [2.7m]
□	Flesh Tone	–	#56	½ yd. [0.5m]
■	Holly	#31	#27	½ yd. [0.5m]

STITCH KEY:
— Backstitch/Straight
● French Knot

Speed Skater Santa
(cut 1) 29 x 30 holes

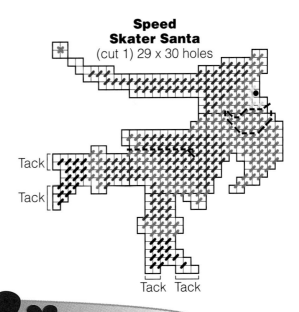

Tack

Tack

Tack Tack

Heartwarming Story

At the age of seven, I had one thing on my mind for Christmas – a pair of skates. I asked my parents if I could have a pair, but they couldn't promise anything, so I took my appeal to Santa. I wrote out my list of things I'd dearly love for Christmas, and at the top of that list were skates. For the whole month of December I ate, slept and breathed skates. When the day finally arrived, I had opened all my packages under the tree and none contained my long-awaited treasures. Sure, I was thankful for all the other nice gifts I received, like a pogo stick and an easy-bake oven, but the skates were the dearest to my heart. Later, my mother found me alone and handed me the most beautifully-wrapped package from behind her back. She hugged me and told me the gift was because I was so special. I tore open that wrapping paper feverishly, and inside, I found snowy-white skates with shiny steel wheels. My mom had even made bright red pom-poms to top off the laces. After much use, I eventually outgrew those skates and passed them on to my little sister. Then, she too outgrew them and the skates were retired from our childhood. Now, they are safely tucked away in my grandmother's attic, waiting to be taken out and appreciated for all the fond memories they hold. – Salway Sabri

General Instructions

Most plastic canvas stitchers love getting their projects organized before they even step out the door in search of supplies. A few moments of careful planning can make the creation of your project even more fun.

First of all, prepare your work area. You will need a flat surface for cutting and assembly, and you will need a place to store your materials. Good lighting is essential, and a comfortable chair will make your stitching time even more enjoyable.

Do you plan to make one project, or will you be making several of the same item? A materials list appears at the beginning of each pattern. If you plan to make several of the same item, multiply your materials accordingly.

Each project features U. S. standard and metric measurements.

> **METRIC KEY:**
>
> millimeters = [mm]
> centimeters = [cm]
> meters = [m]
> grams = [g]

Supplies

Yarn, canvas, needles, cutters and most other supplies needed to complete the projects in this book are available through craft and needlework stores and mail order catalogs. Other supplies are available at fabric, hardware and discount stores.

Canvas

Most projects can be made using standard-size sheets of canvas. Standard-size sheets of 7-count (7 holes per inch) are 70 x 90 holes and are about 10½" x 13½" [26.7cm x 34.3cm]. For larger projects, 7-count canvas also comes in 12" x 18" [30.5cm x 45.7cm] (80 x 120 holes) and 13½" x 22½" [34.3cm x 57.2cm] (90 x 150 holes) sheets. Other shapes are available in 7-count, including circles, diamonds, ovals and purse forms.

10-count canvas (10 holes per inch) comes only in standard-size sheets, which vary slightly depending on brand. They are 10½" x 13½" [26.7cm x 34.3cm] (106 x 136 holes) or 11" x 14" [27.9cm x 35.6cm] (108 x 138 holes).

5-count canvas (5 holes per inch) and 14-count (14 holes per inch) sheets are also available.

Some canvas is soft and pliable, while other canvas is stiffer and more rigid. To prevent canvas from cracking during or after stitching, you'll want to choose pliable canvas for projects that require shaping, like round baskets with curved handles. For easier shaping, warm canvas pieces with a blow-dry hair dryer to soften; dip in cool water to set. If your project is a box or an item that will stand alone, stiffer canvas is more suitable.

Both 7- and 10-count canvas are available in a rainbow of colors. Most designs can be stitched on colored as well as clear canvas. When a pattern does not specify a color in the materials list, you can assume clear canvas was used in the photographed model. If you'd like to stitch only a portion of the design, leaving a portion unstitched, use colored canvas to coordinate with yarn colors.

Buy the same brand of canvas for each entire project.

Yarn & Other Stitching Materials

You may choose two-ply nylon plastic canvas yarn (the color numbers of two popular brands are found in the Color Keys) or four-ply worsted-weight yarn for stitching on 7-count canvas. There are about 42 yards per ounce of plastic canvas yarn and 50 yards per ounce of worsted-weight yarn.

Worsted-weight yarn is widely available and comes in wool, acrylic, cotton and blends. If you decide to use worsted-weight yarn, choose 100% acrylic for best coverage. Select worsted-weight yarn by color instead of the color names or numbers found in the Color Keys. Projects stitched with worsted-weight yarn often "fuzz" after use. "Fuzz" can be removed by shaving with a fabric shaver to make your project look new again.

Plastic canvas yarn comes in over 67 colors. These yarns "wear" well both while stitching and in the finished product. When buying plastic canvas yarn, shop using the color names or numbers found in the Color Keys, or select colors of your choice.

Metallic cord is as tightly-woven cord that comes in dozens of glittering colors. If your metallic cord has a white core, the core may be removed for easier stitching.

Cutting Tools

You may find it helpful to have several tools on hand for cutting canvas. When cutting long, straight sections, scissors, craft cutters or kitchen shears are the fastest and easiest to use. For cutting out detailed areas and trimming nubs, you may like using manicure scissors, nail clippers or the Ultimate Plastic Canvas Cutters, available only from *The Needlecraft Shop* catalog (see address on page 157). If you prefer laying your canvas flat when cutting, try a craft knife and cutting surface — self-healing mats designed for sewing, and kitchen cutting boards work well.

Needles & Other Stitching Tools

Blunt-end tapestry needles are used for stitching plastic canvas. Choose a No. 16 needle for stitching 5- and 7-count, a No. 18 for stitching 10-count, and a No. 24 for stitching 14-count. Keep a small pair of embroidery scissors handy for snipping yarn. Try using needle-nose jewelry pliers for pulling the needle through several thicknesses of canvas and out of tight spots too small for your hand.

Marking & Cutting Canvas

To avoid wasting canvas, careful cutting of each piece is important. For some pieces with square corners, you might be comfortable cutting the canvas without marking it beforehand. But for pieces with lots of angles and cutouts, you may want to mark your canvas before cutting.

To count holes on the graphs, look for the bolder lines showing each ten holes. These ten-count lines begin in the lower left-hand corner of each graph and are on the graph to make counting easier. To count holes on the canvas, you may use your tapestry needle, a toothpick or a plastic hair roller pick. Insert the needle or pick slightly in each hole as you count.

Most stitchers have tried a variety of marking tools and have settled on a favorite, which may be crayon, permanent marker or grease pencil. One of the best marking tools is a fine-point overhead projection marker, available at office supply stores. The ink is dark and easy to see and washes off completely with water. After cutting and before stitching, it's important to remove all marks so they won't stain yarn as you stitch or show through stitches later. Cloth and paper toweling remove grease pencil and crayon marks, as do used fabric softener sheets.

Follow all Cutting Instructions, Notes and labels above graphs to cut canvas. Each piece is labeled with a letter of the alphabet. Square-sided pieces are cut according to hole count, and some may not have graphs.

Unlike sewing patterns, graphs are not designed to be used as actual patterns but rather as counting, cutting and stitching guides. Therefore, graphs may not be actual size. Count the holes on the graph, mark your canvas to match, then cut. Trim off the nubs close to the bar, and trim all corners diagonally.

If you accidentally cut or tear a bar or two on your canvas, don't worry! Boo-boos can usually be repaired in one of several ways: heat the tip of a metal skewer and melt the canvas back together; glue torn bars with a tiny drop of craft glue, Super Glue® or hot glue; or reinforce the torn section with a separate piece of canvas placed at the back of your work. When reinforcing with extra canvas, stitch through both thicknesses.

Stitching the Canvas

Stitching Instructions for each section are found after the Cutting Instructions. First, refer to the illustrations of basic stitches on page 159 to familiarize yourself with the stitches used. Illustrations will be found near the graphs for pieces worked using special stitches. Follow the numbers on the tiny graph beside the illustration to make each stitch — bring your needle up from the back of the work on odd numbers and down through the front of the work on the even numbers.

Before beginning, read the Stitching Instructions to get an overview of what you'll be doing. You'll find that some pieces are stitched using colors and stitches indicated on graphs, and for other pieces you will be told which color and stitch to use to cover the entire piece.

Cut yarn lengths no longer than 18" [45.7cm] to prevent fraying. Thread needle; do not tie a knot in the end. Bring your needle up through the canvas from the back, leaving a short length of yarn on the wrong side of the canvas. As you begin to stitch, work over this short length of yarn. If you are beginning with Continental Stitches, leave a 1" [2.5cm] length, but if you are working longer stitches, leave a longer length.

In order for graph colors to contrast well, graph colors may not match yarn colors. For instance, a light yellow may have been selected to represent the metallic cord color gold, or a light blue may represent white yarn.

When following a graph showing several colors, you may want to work all the stitches of one color at the same time. Some stitchers prefer to work with several colors at once by threading each on a separate needle and letting the yarn not being used hang on the wrong side of the work. Either way, remember that strands of yarn run across the

wrong side of the work may show through the stitches from the front.

As you stitch, try to maintain an even tension on the yarn. Loose stitches will look uneven, and tight stitches will let the canvas show through. If your yarn twists as you work, you may want to let your needle and yarn hang and untwist occasionally.

When you end a section of stitching or finish a thread, weave the yarn through the back side of your last few stitches, then trim it off.

Construction & Assembly

After all pieces of an item needing assembly are stitched, you will find the order of assembly is listed in the Stitching Instructions and sometimes illustrated in diagrams found with the graphs. For best results, join pieces in the order written. Refer to the Stitch Key and to the directives near the graphs for precise attachments.

Finishing Tips

To combat glue strings when using a hot glue gun, practice a swirling motion as you work. After placing the drop of glue on your work, lift the gun slightly and swirl to break the stream of glue, as if you were making an ice cream cone. Have a cup of water handy when gluing. For those times when you'll need to touch the glue, first dip your finger into the water just enough to dampen it. This will minimize the glue sticking to your finger, and it will cool and set the glue more quickly.

To attach beads, use a bit more glue to form a cup around the bead. If too much shows after drying, use a craft knife to trim off excess glue.

Scotchguard® or other fabric protectors may be used on your finished projects. However, avoid using a permanent marker if you plan to use a fabric protector, and be sure to remove all other markings before stitching. Fabric protectors can cause markings to bleed, staining yarn.

For More Information

If you have difficulty completing your project, write to Plastic Canvas Editors, *The Needlecraft Shop*, 23 Old Pecan Road, Big Sandy, Texas 75755.

Acknowledgments

Fireside Comforts for the Family

Darice®: Plastic Canvas for Christmas Classic, Snowman Wall Basket, Mug Inserts.

Uniek®: Needloft Yarn for Poinsettia Bells, Christmas Classic. Metallic Cord for Poinsettia Bells.

DMC®: Pearl Cotton for Christmas Classic, Mug Inserts. Embroidery floss for Fireplace Card Holder.

Coats & Clark: Red Heart yarn for Snowman Wall Basket, North Pole Tissues.

Aunt Lydia's: Yarn for Snowman Wall Basket.

Natura: Yarn for Snowman Wall Basket.

Charles Craft: E-Z Stitch Mugs for Mug Inserts.

Lasting Memories for Your Best Friend

Darice®: Plastic Canvas for Frosty Photo Fun, Waiting for Santa, Wedding Dreams. Metallic Cord for Wedding Dreams.

Uniek®: Needloft Yarn for Frosty Photo Fun, Waiting for Santa Tote, Wedding Dreams, May Flower Medley, Winter Gift Box.

DMC®: Pearl Cotton for Winter Gift Box, Waiting for Santa.

Loving Touches for the Romantics

Darice®: Plastic Canvas for Lace & Roses Bath, Sweetheart Scents, Hearts & Crosses. Nylon Plus Yarn for Sweetheart Scents.

Uniek®: Needloft Yarn for Lace & Roses Bath, To My Love.

DMC®: Pearl Cotton for To My Love.

Coats & Clark: Red Heart Yarn for Ribbon Rose Box.

Aleene's®: Glue for Lace & Roses Bathroom Set, Hearts & Crosses Bridal Set.

Wright's®: Trim & Lace for Lace & Roses Bath, Hearts & Crosses.

Bucilla®: Silk Trim for Ribbon Rose Box.

Novtex Corporation: Trim for Hearts & Crosses.

Tasty Creations for the Cook

Darice®: Plastic Canvas for Fruit Gift Basket, Bee Suncatcher. Nylon Plus Yarn for Bee Suncatcher. Bright Pearls Lustre Cord for Bee Suncatcher.

Uniek®: Needloft Yarn for Fruit Gift Basket, Goodie Baskets. Metallic Cord for Goodie Baskets.

Caron®: Christmas Glitter Yarn for Glittery Accents.

Day Brighteners for Your Co-Workers

Darice®: Plastic Canvas for Holiday Shelf Sitters, Winter Welcome, Merry Elf. Nylon Plus Yarn for Holiday Shelf Sitters.

Uniek®: Needloft Yarn for Winter Welcome.

DMC®: Pearl Cotton for Winter Welcome, Merry Elf. Embroidery Floss for Holiday Shelf Sitters.

Coats & Clark: Red Heart Classic & Super Saver Yarn for Merry Elf.

Aleene's®: Glue for Merry Elf.

The Beadery®: Acrylic Gems for Holiday Shelf Sitters.

Kreinik: Metallic Braid for Merry Elf.

JHB: Buttons for Merry Elf.

All Cooped Up Designs™: Stringlets Doll Hair for Merry Elf.

Simple Pleasures for Special People

Darice®: Plastic Canvas for Praying Hands, School Bus, Mini Folk Stockings, Holiday Pins, Bejeweled Baskets. Nylon Plus Yarn for Mini Folk Stockings.

Uniek®: Needloft Yarn for Sweet Faces Coasters, Praying Hands, School Bus, Baking Cups.

DMC®: Pearl Cotton for School Bus, Holiday Pins. Embroidery Floss for Sweet Faces Coasters, Baking Cups.

Anchor®: Embroidery Floss for Praying Hands.

Aleene's®: Glue for Holiday Pins, Bejeweled Baskets.

Offray: Ribbon for Sweet Faces Coasters.

Kreinik: Metallic Ribbon for Holiday Pins.

The Beadery®: Gemstones for Bejewled Baskets

Growing Traditions for the Gardener

Darice®: Plastic Canvas for Birdie Welcome, Bumble Bee Bookend, Garden Angel, Bird Nest Box, Crescent Moon Santa, Snowbirds Window.

Uniek®: Needloft Yarn for Bee Bookend, Garden Angel, Bow Planter Set.

DMC®: Pearl Cotton for Bumble Bee Bookend, Birdie Welcome, Garden Angel, Crescent Moon Santa, Snowbirds Window.

Coats & Clark: Red Heart Classic & Super Saver Yarn for Birdie Welcome, Bird Nest Box, Snowbirds Window.

Aleene's®: Glue for Birdie Welcome, Bird Nest Box, Crescent Moon Santa, Snowbirds Window.

Mill Hill: Gay Bowles Sales, Inc., Glass Pebble Beads for Garden Angel.

Spinrite®: Plastic Canvas Yarn for Crescent Moon Santa.

Kreinik: Metallic Braid for Crescent Moon Santa.

JHB: Cardinal Buttons #90031 for Snowbirds Window.

Photography Credits

A special thanks to models Micah Godfrey and Amber Beal; Prop help from Julie Wilkins, *Annies Tea Room* and Rudy Beloney, Big Sandy, Texas

Stitch Guide

NEEDLEPOINT STITCHES

CONTINENTAL
can be used to stitch designs or fill in background areas.

WHIPSTITCH
is used to join two or more pieces together.

LONG
is a horizontal or vertical stitch used to stitch designs or fill in background areas. Can be stitched over two or more bars.

CROSSED OVERCAST

MOSAIC

HERRINGBONE OVERCAST

OVERCAST
is used to finish edges. Stitch two or three times in corners for complete coverage.

CROSSED WHIPSTITCH

HERRINGBONE WHIPSTITCH

SCOTCH

SLANTED GOBELIN
can be used to stitch designs or fill in background areas. Can be stitched over two or more bars in vertical or horizontal rows.

EMBROIDERY STITCHES

BACKSTITCH
is usually used as an embroidery stitch to outline or add detail. Stitches can be any length and go in any direction.

CROSS
can be used as a needlepoint stitch or as an embroidery stitch stitched over background stitches with contrasting yarn or floss.

LARK'S HEAD

FRENCH KNOT
is usually used as an embroidery stitch to add detail. Can be made in one hole or over a bar. If dot on graph is in hole, come up and go down with needle in same hole. If dot is across a bar or over grid, come up in one hole and go down one hole over.

MODIFIED TURKEY WORK
is used to fill in background areas or as an embroidery stitch to add a loopy or fringed texture. Stitch over one bar leaving a loop, then stitch over the same bar to anchor the loop.

LAZY DAISY
is usually used as an embroidery stitch to add detail. Can be any length and go in any direction. Come up and go down in same hole, leaving loop. Come up in another hole for top of stitch, put needle through loop and go down in same hole.

SMYRNA CROSS
can be used as a needlepoint stitch or as an embroidery stitch, stitched over background stitches with contrasting yarn or floss.

STRAIGHT
is usually used as an embroidery stitch to add detail. Stitches can be any length and can go in any direction. Looks like Backstitch except stitches do not touch.

159

Pattern Index

Designer Index